FOR OVER 20 YEARS

Lauren Mote has tended bars and traveled the world, developing cocktail recipes, seeking out new ingredients, and gathering stories along the way. Now, in her first book, Lauren is inviting readers and home bartenders to pack their suitcases and come with her on an international cocktail adventure.

Few bartenders can match Lauren's encyclopedic knowledge of spirits, liqueurs, and tinctures, not to mention her originality for blending them into a perfectly-balanced drink. Once you've gotten a handle on the basics of bartending, and gathered your cocktail shaker along with a few other pieces of equipment, you'll be raising your glass in no time.

The recipes are organized by their star ingredients, such as agave, gin, whiskey, rum, vodka, and more. Every drink is given its own designation of standard, mid, low, or zero proof, and you'll find a whole chapter on nonalcoholic cocktails, because Lauren feels strongly that all drinks should be prepared with care, whether they include alcohol or not. Once you've narrowed down the base that you're in the mood for, let Lauren's magnetic storytelling and gift of the gab continue to guide you. Want a drink inspired by the Old Fashioned that will transport you to the sea cliffs of County Cork, Ireland? Try the Apple-ation. For a Hawaiian interpretation of a Vodka Sour, with flavors of coconut, flowers, and citrus, try the Sour Roses. Or if you're looking for a nonalcoholic beverage that will quench your thirst and delight your palate, try the Greenish, which is Lauren's zero proof take on the Collins, and inspired by her travels to Hong Kong. In each chapter, you'll find a collection of Mise en Place Recipes to help you build up your bar's basic ingredients and make Lauren's techniques your own.

With beautiful storytelling and photography, and cocktail recipes you won't find elsewhere, *A Bartender's Guide to the World* is as much a pleasure to read as it is to imbibe from. Grab your glass and let's go!

A BARTENDER'S GUIDE TO THE WORLD

A BARTENDER'S GUIDE TO THE WORLD

Cocktails and Stories
from 75 Places

LAUREN MOTE

and James O. Fraioli

appetite
by RANDOM HOUSE

Appetite by Random House® and colophon are
registered trademarks of Penguin Random House LLC.

Library and Archives of Canada Cataloguing in
Publication is available upon request.

ISBN: 9780525611295
eBook ISBN: 9780525611301

Cover and book design by Terri Nimmo
Cover and book photography by Jonathan Chovancek
Printed in China

Published in Canada by Appetite by Random House®,
a division of Penguin Random House LLC.

www.penguinrandomhouse.ca

10 9 8 7 6 5 4 3 2 1

This book is dedicated to Jonathan, my husband and chop, and Linda, the mothership. Thank you for supporting my dream during the grim and grand moments alike. The book is also dedicated to bartenders. Bartenders can change the world. All my life I wanted to share stories, drinks, flavors, and friendships, and bartending made that possible.

CONTENTS

Foreword by Lynnette Marrero   1

Introduction:

    2 Decades & 75 Places   3

Getting Started   9

    Setting Up Your Home Bar   9

    Stocking Up   9

    My Top 12 Specialty Ingredients   14

    Equipment, Tools & Accessories   16

    Understanding Proof & ABV   21

Cocktail Design   23

    Regional Inspiration   23

    Bartending Basics   23

Agave Spirits   27

Brandy   49

Gin   69

Liqueur & Amaro   97

Rum   115

Vodka   135

Whiskey   161

Wine   187

Zero Proof   217

Nonalcoholic & Alcoholic

    Vermouths   235

Acknowledgments   241

Index   242

FOREWORD
BY LYNNETTE MARRERO

I met Lauren Mote via email in 2013 through a mutual industry connection. Lauren's note told me a few things immediately: not only that she was committed to the advancement of her Canadian bar community, she was fearless, and she was a doer, but also that she was seeking a global connection and community.

At the time, I was running the New York City chapter of LUPEC (Ladies United for the Preservation of Endangered Cocktails), and Lauren wanted to start a chapter in Canada to expand on the work she was already doing to provide a more unified education for her national bar community. We met later that summer at Tales of the Cocktail in New Orleans, and our connection was immediate. Lauren is a strikingly tall woman whose presence is immediately felt in any room she enters. What really grabs your attention are her intensity, focus, and true investment in the people with whom she engages. I had no idea at this point how influential she would be in my bartending life.

The following year, Lauren led a pilgrimage of Canadian women bartenders to Seattle to compete in Speed Rack, an all-women's cocktail bar competition that I had started with my partner, Ivy Mix. We had never before included international bartenders in the US National competition, and the following year, Lauren took on the intense responsibility of launching the Speed Rack Canada competition in Vancouver.

Engaging with Lauren's entrepreneurial spirit has been one of the most inspiring parts of our friendship. She and her partner, Jonathan, have built and grown one of the best craft bitters companies in the world; their bitters provided my first interaction with her incredible palate and sense of flavor pairing. Her ability to fuse global culinary flavors into beautiful, balanced cocktails is incredible. I watched with admiration as she created her own role as the Diageo "Global Cocktailian," a position only someone as tenacious as Lauren could pitch and sell.

The last few years, my meet-ups with Lauren have taken place in numerous cities all over the world, from Hawaii to London, Germany to Brazil. I have watched her build connections around the globe, and I have seen the wonderful influences in her work.

In this book, Lauren is like an investigative journalist, sharing stories about the places she has visited and, more importantly, about what she has gained from her connection to the people there. After finishing this book, you will have an understanding of the cocktail journey of each locale—its style, flavor profiles, cultural references, and historical references. You will discover Lauren's passion for building bridges and connections with bartenders around the world.

So book your around-the-world ticket and travel with *A Bartender's Guide to the World*, where every recipe will transport you to a unique time and place.

Lynnette Marrero
Cofounder of Speed Rack
Mixology Teacher, Masterclass.com
Winner of the Altos Bartender's Bartender Award, 2021

INTRODUCTION
2 DECADES
& 75 PLACES

I'm Lauren Mote, an award-winning bartender and multiple business owner in the drinks industry. Over the past two decades, I have worked many styles of bars and restaurants in Canada, from dive bars and neighborhood joints to Relais & Châteaux properties and the Four Seasons hotel group. I've represented some of the greatest spirits on the planet. In the earlier part of my career, I focused on getting myself through school with jobs in food and beverages before homing in on the industry as my full-time passion. I've competed and won international bartending competitions, including World Class Canada and the Grey Goose Iconoclasts series. I've developed training programs for Grand Marnier, Heering, Laphroaig, and Chartreuse, and have received accolades from *Vancouver* magazine, Tales of the Cocktail, the Dame Hall of Fame, and Drinks International. I've traveled the world—over fifty countries—and I'm constantly in awe with every discovery of a new flavor, a local custom, and the people behind them. Today, I'm the co-owner of an award-winning, internationally distributed cocktail bitters company, Bittered Sling, founded in 2012 with my husband, Chef Jonathan Chovancek, and we also own a marketing and photography consulting agency here in Europe. I am a sommelier, writer, and spirits educator, as well as the first woman to win World Class Canada before competing at the World Class Global Final in South Africa in 2015, placing in the top twelve globally. Over the last decade, I have represented some of the best spirits in the world, traveling to far flung regions, developing relationships with and education for bartenders of every experience level.

In this book, I'm proud to share stories that have helped me form my positive outlook on the drinks industry over the last two decades. Each story is illustrated with a cocktail that perfectly brings the scene to life, because after all, deliciousness is best experienced from all the senses. But first, my own story.

I grew up in downtown Toronto. My mom was a single mother of three kids who was putting herself through night school to get a better job. This didn't leave a lot of money for food, so we often ate canned foods—sometimes from the food bank—along with simple salads, soups, and pasta. That was it. But with great enthusiasm and a spice rack of flavors, Mom made the most of the situation. Generally, I would see my dad at my grandmother Rose's house for random meals. My brothers, Jake and Sasha, and I would get to enjoy the greatest hits of Forest Hill's awesome Jewish delis: chopped liver, roasted chicken, matzoh ball soup, kishke, you name it. At my British grandmother Florence's house, we'd devour homemade party foods, from sandwiches and teatime snacks to a huge roast with a thousand sides, and a dessert course that was even larger than the main: trifle, bread pudding, custards, and more.

Over the years, I would stand at my grandmothers' side while they cooked. I know this is cliché—yes, another story about grandmothers cooking—but the foods they exposed me to changed my life. Food wasn't just something required for energy; it was everything. It was the entertainment, the creativity, the calculated recipe creations. I loved it all. At a very young age I stopped socializing with my family in the living room and helped in the kitchen. We'd celebrate later, watching *The Simpsons* and eating Cadbury chocolates with my Auntie Carol. These meals linked me to two very different sides of my family—my ancestral homes, the lands we came from, the

dream—it was my therapy as a teenager and well into my twenties.

My first experience with alcohol as a young adult was a $3.85 bottle of Olde English malt liquor with my pals from school. I remember the awkward moment sitting outside the school portables in the Beaches neighborhood of Toronto, having my first sip and being absolutely disgusted. "Is this what I've been waiting for? *Gross.*" After trying a few more sips, I

I started bartending because I longed to feel part of a family.

traditions of our past—all handed down over the ages on the plate and in the most memorable places. I would find recipes for burdock wine written on the back of grocery receipts or cocktail napkins from a long-ago soirée, preserved in the stacks of old *TV Guide* magazines, or the scribbled recipes for poppyseed moon cookies in my great-grandmother's diary, which she published in 1994, on her 100th birthday, for the entire family to read. I cherish my copy.

I was destined to end up in food and drinks, because that's what made me happiest. And I needed the distraction. I was often bullied during this time, first for not being Jewish enough in one neighborhood, and then for being too Jewish when we moved to a new area. My salvation was cooking, and my biggest reward was the smiles on people's faces as they ate my creations. When I was eighteen, I opened a catering company called Mademoiselle Chef to support my

figured the feeling was worth the horrific taste. When I found my mom's stash of mixto tequila and my uncle's spiced rum, the flavors improved, but not that much. I longed for the togetherness, and what looked like happiness, that my mom, stepdad, and their friends enjoyed around the dining room table after we went to sleep. I listened from the staircase late at night to crazy stories of adventures and general chitchat, complemented by billows of smoke and the sound of wine corks popping and glasses clinking late into the night. Wine was instantly interesting to me—the thousands of wine labels were rooted in culture and heritage from far-flung places around the world. I also hoped that the more I learned about wine and food, the more I was destined to meet other people like me.

After high school, I took two years off and worked a number of jobs to learn as much as I could. I had the gift for gab and the ability to listen and contribute at a high level—and a photographic memory to boot! I was a strong public speaker, comedic, creative, and energetic. When I took my first bar job at eighteen, I was able to bring all of these traits, as well as my understanding of people, customer service, passion for flavors, and excellent time management together. I saw it all as a swan dance with a lot of mathematics on the business side, and I loved the challenge and triumph of finishing a service of endless chits, delivering perfect drinks in a timely fashion, chatting with and entertaining my guests, taking orders, and settling payments, all simultaneously.

One night, after several lychee martinis at Hey Lucy in Toronto, I had an epiphany: I was ready for a new adventure. I decided to go to university and wound up at the University of Waterloo, and then Toronto, studying and attending classes during the day, and working at night at Le Select Bistro, a high-end, popular restaurant in downtown Toronto. But the academic honeymoon didn't last—school was complicated and my job was amazing. I wasn't living at home, and the pressure at school was heavy. I couldn't really relate to anyone there, either. I relied heavily on the family of misfits at work who made me feel so comfortable. They challenged me on a different level, and I blossomed into an even more eccentric version of myself. I felt like I had arrived.

I'll always remember standing on the university campus, with the bright sunshine beaming down on me, on the phone with my mom, bawling my eyes out at the thought of leaving school. It felt like I had failed. She said, "Lauren, you're brilliant and talented, and being happy is far more important than being tormented. You're obviously meant to do something else. These are lessons, expensive lessons, that you needed to learn the hard way. We all do." (For more about my mom's awesomeness, see Dancing Queen on page 128.)

Over the next year, I took my $45,000 in student loans, made a new plan, and hit the road west for Vancouver.

In 2010 I met my now-husband, Jonathan Chovancek. It was love at first sight and first conversation. Jonathan was an accomplished chef, and the possibilities for two young gastronomy-obsessed lovers like us were wide open. We opened two companies, Kale & Nori Culinary Arts (a boutique catering and events company) and Bittered Sling (our cocktail bitters company). Within the first year of dating, we blended our lives, cutlery, and cookbook collections and set about bringing our vision of great food and beverage culture to life through events across Canada and around the world.

It's such a blur, but fast-forward to 2019, when, with over 600 books in our shipping container, we moved across the ocean from Canada to the Netherlands to live in Amsterdam for a new adventure. Our library has helped us define our journey, and books have become markers on our timelines, always bringing us back to a certain place or event. Hard-cover encyclopedias and reference books; philosophy texts; atlases of both geographical and wine regions; food science tomes; books about cooking, drinks, foraging, and farming. They feed my obsession with the oceans, mountains, outer space, and the unknown cosmos, as well as my love of color synesthesia (the psychology of color), art history, and fragrances. I've always wanted to write a book that captured my journey on paper—I don't want to forget the special moments that shaped my life.

I started bartending because I longed to feel like part of a family, one whose members accepted me unconditionally. Over the last two decades, I have been a college and university student, a song-writer/burger-dresser, a bookkeeper, a server, a bartender, a hostess, a somme-lier, a cook, a caterer, an event planner, a (multiple) business owner, a manager, a marketer, a consultant, a writer, an educator and a mentor. The road to this point has swayed from side to side—a clear path on some days, roadblocked on others—but each role and experience added to my toolbox. I love the challenges around every corner and, more impor-tantly, the treasure trove of people I've met along the way. It's the courage to fail as well as succeed that's allowed me the opportunity to shine in my different roles, expand and evolve existing positions, and broaden the scope of my process, both creatively and analytically. My bartending, storytelling, and cocktail-making style is an amalgamation of all of it. And each person I meet is an amalgamation of their experiences and personality, making each interaction with each person so special. It's my honor to chronicle these moments with a drink, a story, a recipe, and a tribute.

The stories in these pages are an amalgamation of key moments from my last twenty years, including a few from 2020, the year we are still trying to make sense of. It was a complicated year for many reasons, not least of which was a global pandemic. I saw friends and colleagues struggle and lose so much, and others find beauty and calmness in the chaos. As I write this, the pandemic continues, and impacts everything we do. But through it all, my community has stayed together and grown stronger. Their perseverance has pushed me to move faster and work harder in the moments when it was most challenging. Blending and creating flavors is my life, but developing friendships through flavor is my life's work.

Bartenders are in the business of serving at the pleasure of their guests and teammates, while making drinks on time and on budget. Please support local bars, restaurants, and businesses where possible—from those who provide you with the beautiful products to make the drinks to the neighborhood bar and the local coffee roaster.

This book is meant to take you away on a journey to flavor town, inspired by my travels as a bartender and with bartenders around the world. From central meeting places, cafés, and social events, socializing, food, and drink, what I've learned is that great conversations and good company are the zest of life and the very essence of our being. Cocktail making doesn't have to be complicated. In fact, serving a light highball with delicious snacks, vacation-inspired drinks midweek, or ice cream floats and zero-proof spritzes are all part of having fun. You choose the occasion, and I'll provide the recipe and feel-good story that brings it all together.

Lauren

GETTING STARTED

The book is as much about storytelling as it is about cocktails and flavor. They are intrinsically connected, and my career has been defined by my ability to be not only a great host and entertainer, but also a student and teacher. Each chapter is organized by base ingredient—traditional cocktail ingredients include spirits, aromatized wines, and liqueurs, while non-traditional ingredients take us into a different realm with nuts, tubers, flowers, and vegetables. There's a nonalcoholic, or "NA," focus to ensure I am being true to the direction my life is taking, and to be inclusive of all bartenders and their guests who feel the same.

Before we get into the nitty-gritty, we need to talk through a few best practices to get you started, and set up for success.

Setting Up Your Home Bar

To make great drinks, you need great tools. You don't have to go overboard and get all the fancy equipment; start with the basics and work in new items over time. I often scour local thrift stores and secondhand shops to find vintage glasses, mixing tins, unique and beautiful spoons, and, if I am lucky, some kick-ass enamel containers!

I've seen home bars put together in different ways—bar carts, cupboards, and milk crate castles can all work—but the most important thing is having easy access to your bar tools; otherwise, you might not make drinks as often as you'd like. While I don't store all my bar tools next to my cutlery, I always have a jigger on hand and a bar spoon and shaker close by. Storing the mixing glass next to your glassware allows easy access. And get a few fancy ice molds and always have a ziplock bag of ice ready to go (there is nothing worse than craving a cocktail and not having any ice). We store our bitters collection in the same place as our spices; after all, bitters are the salt and pepper of the drinks world. Try to blend the food and drink worlds together in your home, and it will become habitual to make cocktails. How do you do this? Keep reading.

Stocking Up

Today we have access to a huge selection of products from all over the world, accessible at any time of the year. I like to work with in-season fruits and vegetables whenever possible, but I also use a wide range of products from other countries. When you're deciding which products to buy, the quality of the spirit or brand, the flavor, and the price point are all important considerations, but also use your buying power to look for brands that:

- support communities, whether local or global;
- make a commitment to their employees and the environment;
- invest in the future of the bartending profession and the hospitality industry;
- have a rich, authentic story and heritage; and
- showcase outstanding craftsmanship.

Ultimately, the better your base spirits and modifiers are, the better your drinks will be. Here are a few notes for each category, to set you up for success:

Agave Spirits

Choosing tequila can be quite simple. Blanco tequilas are young and fresh, with no oak maturation, and have a wide range of tasting notes, from citrus to white or bell pepper to grassy notes. Reposado is "rested" for a minimum of six months in oak, softening the freshness into more toasted notes, like coconut and caramel. Añejo (rested for at least one year) and extra añejo (rested for at least two years) and represent some of the most luxurious aromas, flavors, and finishes, giving us great opportunities to consume them neat, in dessert drinks and digestifs. Whichever style is called for, be sure to choose 100% blue agave tequilas. Avoid mixtos (51% agave), which can include distillates not necessarily derived from the agave plant to make up the other 49%. This can result in unwanted sweetness or fishy and skunky flavors and aromas. The expression of 100% blue agave is fresh, crisp, and clean.

The jump from tequila to mezcal is like going from a honeyed Highland scotch to a peated Islay whisky. There are many directions to explore, with hundreds of agaves in production. I recommend starting with something soft and approachable with a more vegetal, earthy, and slightly smoky nose and palate, such as an Espadín, Tobalá, or Madrecuixe agave. Agave spirits are my favorites!

Brandy

From pisco to cognac, Armagnac, Calvados, and other fruit brandies and eaux de vies, there are lots to choose from, so focus on great producers that highlight their base materials and process on the bottle or their website. The aromas should be robust yet delicate, floral, and well spiced, evocative of the fruit in the base, whether that's grapes, apples, pears, strawberries, cherries, grape skins and pits, raspberries, or beyond. The palate should be bone dry, with a smooth, long-lasting finish. Eaux de vies are great to have on hand in small bottles to accent and modify drink recipes—you'll see that a lot in this book, as they're my secret weapon. Spanish, French, and other regional brandies are delightful, using various grapes with different flavor profiles. Rating systems like VS (very special), VSOP (very superior old pale), and XO (extra old) help to capture a quality standard in regions such as Cognac.

Gin

This spirit is produced all over the world, giving us a breadth of variety. I recommend starting with mini bottles of different types if you're fairly unfamiliar with the category. London dry gins should be beaming with juniper flavor on the nose and palate, supported with citrus and spice notes, but each brand and distillery will have its own signature style. Local and craft distilleries will produce gins and sell them while their whiskies and rums are aging away in barrels. There are no spices that are taboo, so have some fun with these bottles.

Genever is a cool category to discover. It's the ancestor of gin as we know it, originating in Belgium and the Netherlands, with deep roots as a malted barley spirit with juniper extract added for its health benefit. Genever gin is centuries old, predating London dry gins, and holds a special place in the hearts of those who study historical spirits. Hundreds of varieties exist in the European market, and Genever is gradually making its way into the global marketplace.

I'll stick aquavit in here too—while it's not a gin, it's a neutral spirit that, like gin, is influenced by different botanicals, with a heavy emphasis on caraway seeds as the dominant flavor. Aquavit (or akvavit) is the ultimate expression of the Nordics. The flavors are brilliant and rich, so a little goes a long way when you're trying it for the first time. As with craft gin, many distilleries are making their own local versions of this unique spirit. I would take the same approach as for mezcal and start with an easygoing bottle like Brennivín or Linie.

Liqueur & Amaro

There is seldom an appropriate replacement for the specific liqueur or amaro recommended in a recipe, so use the "call brand" mentioned. For liqueurs, my irreplaceable favorites are Chartreuse and Bénédictine, from centuries-old recipes produced in monasteries in France. Amari flavors range from rhubarb-focused to herbal and wintery to bright and zesty.

Rum

This is an exciting category of styles, flavors, and regional representation. As with gins, I recommend purchasing mini bottles of different styles and brands to discover. Agricole rums (from French Caribbean islands) and cachaça (from Brazil) are made from pressed cane juice, whereas Spanish and English rums are centered around molasses. White, amber, and aged rums can be made from either cane juice or molasses; what changes is the time they spend in barrels, and what material the barrels are made from. Aged rums are wonderful on their own and work beautifully in stirred drinks or those cocktails where an oak-matured spirit like cognac or whiskey might be called for.

Vodka

Regions and base materials vary, so experiment with the flavors and bottles that excite you. Compared to other spirit categories, you might feel vodka lacks character, color, aroma, and flavor, but that's part of its beauty. A perfect vodka is easy to spot, as there's nothing in the bottle for it to hide behind. The base material changes the flavor profile, from the light, bright creamy nose of a winter wheat vodka to the earthy, more vegetal (yet soft) tones of potato-based distillates. There are vodkas on the market from virtually all regions of the world, made from any fermentable carbohydrate you can imagine—quinoa, milk, rye, barley, corn. The subtleties of each base material are experienced on the nose and palate. Aromas should be crisp,

vibrant, and pleasant, never reminiscent of gasoline or other "off" fragrances. The palate should be soft and creamy, with a nice long finish. Your tongue should remain wet, with the sides slightly watering. The palate should provide the same, if not a bit more, of what the nose gave you.

Whiskey

The whiskey category is very exciting, with so many styles from different regions available. Whiskies are made from a wide range of grain bases, in unique barrels, guided by different laws. Again, I recommend trying a few mini bottles from various regions: bourbon, American rye whiskey, Canadian whisky, blended scotch, single malts, and Irish whiskey (throw in Japanese and Indian whiskies for good measure, if you're keen). Invest in a great whiskey book with regional styles and brands, and make your own notes once you pop open a bottle and sit with a dram for the first time.

Don't shy away from smoke and peat in scotch whiskies; in fact, run toward them! This signature style from the Scottish west coast and islands brings a flavor profile and balance that just dances on the nose and palate—the ultimate terroir.

Unless it's a staple in your everyday collection, try not to buy the same bottle twice, so you can experience more variety. I love whiskey in cocktails because it's complex and dynamic. It can be light, it can be rich, but it's never dull—we have cask maturation and great distillers and blenders to thank for that.

Wine

When it comes to making cocktails with wine, it's the same principle as for cooking with it: use a wine you'd be happy to drink. As a sommelier, I love to chat through the nuances of different wines from different regions and grapes. Two wineries next door to each other, with the same grapes, will make drastically different versions of the same wine, with just a vein of familiarity provided by the grape's character. A wine atlas helps to give us a visual medium for vineyards and wineries, but like anything else, the key is to choose wines based on premium quality. Different laws, appellations, and grapes can be overwhelming. A great rule of thumb is to choose moderately priced wines with a flavor profile, grape, and region you're keen on, rather than shifting to expensive wines that are not to your taste. This goes for the NA wines for vermouth-making too.

For sake, make your selection based on grade: choose one with a rice-polishing ratio that rubs away many layers of the rice grain. "Junmai" is what you're after on the label.

Sherries are fortified wines from the south of Spain, and the ones called for in this book are easy to find. Fino and manzanilla sherries are bone dry, light, yeasty, and crisp, whereas amontillados are nutty, dark in hue, and rich with umami flavor. Olorosos can be sweet or dry and are incredibly rich. PX or cream sherry gives us the beautiful flavor of a rich sherry with sweetness to balance. Other fortified wines, like Madeira, have a character similar to sherry, with oxidative character. Ports are always sweetened and range from ruby (fruity) to tawny (slightly oxidative and nutty) to vintage (rich, aged, and with special bottlings).

Vermouths are wine-based, aromatized with botanicals, fortified, and often lightly sweetened. As with amaro, the styles, regions, and flavors of vermouth vary. There are great examples to choose from in the dry, white, red, and rosé categories. Standard vermouths like Martini, Cinzano, or Stock are entry-level and work in a pinch, but there are now hundreds of brands available to broaden your horizons. Since they are less than 18% alcohol by volume (ABV), you'll want to drink them within a month, and be sure to store opened bottles in the fridge to prevent oxidation. For home use, I recommend purchasing 16 ounce (500 mL) bottles.

Modifiers, Non-traditional Ingredients & Mise en Place

Liqueurs, bitters, and the other ingredients used in this book are procured over time, so take your time when shopping. Each new bottle or ingredient collected here and there helps build your collection and open up your flavor possibilities. We're in this together for the long game. Liqueurs can often be found in small bottles, so the commitment to coffee, cherry, coconut, peach, and herbal isn't too heavy. Bitters come in very small bottles with a wide range of flavors (like my brand, Bittered Sling bitters), and the blends take the user on a flavorful journey through the barks, roots, spices, and fruits.

My Top 12 Specialty Ingredients

I use some unique ingredients in my cocktail and mise en place recipes, most of which can be found at specialty grocery stores or through online purveyors. Here is a list of twelve ingredients I cannot live without. Procure them over time, and I hope you'll fall in love with them too.

1 **Flowers**: try all edible varieties, including rose, lavender, peony, marigold, and hibiscus.

2 **Raw honeys**: the flowers in each region vary, and bees travel only up to 5 square miles (13 square km) from their hive, so raw honeys are the flavor expression of a particular terroir and its flowers. The potential flavors are endless.

3 **Condensed coconut milk**: this is a great product for those who avoid dairy or anyone who's excited to learn that there's another incredible coconut product on the market. (I am coconut-obsessed!)

7 **Herbs, spices, barks, roots, and other botanicals**: there are so many different spices in my repertoire, and I am bold with them. Whether it's chilies or soft spices, I am all-in for flavor. Some of the unique ingredients found in this book include pink peppercorns, sarsaparilla, vanilla beans, lime leaves, lemongrass, black limes, and pandan leaves.

8 **Essential oils**: You can find pure and organic oils in most health food stores. Essential oils are a great way to administer a controlled amount of aroma. Once open, store them in the fridge. Be very careful to use the recommended amount and specific type called for in a recipe, as they're highly concentrated.

4 Cinchona bark tincture: found in most health food stores, the tincture is a great way to administer a controlled amount of this bitter bark to infusions and vermouths. Once open, store it in the fridge.

9 Store-bought fermented beverages: a wide range of fermented beverages with different flavors and textures, including kombucha, ginger beer, and apple cider, will be available in your market. This book showcases recipes for making tepache and fruit beer.

5 Bittered Sling bitters: I'd be remiss not to mention my own product here. Generally, bitters add depth and complexity to cocktails, both zero proof and standard proof. Bittered Sling bitters are made from 100% non-GMO Canadian grain spirits, and the lineup of expressions is evocative of places we've traveled. Our bitters are sugar-free and coloring-free , made using whole botanicals, water, and alcohol. Add them by the dash.

10 Preserved lemons: a secret weapon for adding a bit of salinity, a touch of brightness, and a hint of *je ne sais quoi*, preserved lemons are magical, both the peels and the brine. Store in the fridge once open.

11 Tiger nuts: these are small tubers, sold whole or ground into meal. It's a unique product that I use in horchata (a traditional Spanish drink) along with rice and almonds. They also make a great plant mylk, for an alternative to dairy.

6 Tea and coffee: I have had the great pleasure over the years to work with tea hunters like Pedro Villalon, and that means my tastes in tea have changed dramatically. Pedro, the owner of O5 Tea in Vancouver, British Columbia, is originally from Mexico, and in addition to being a chemical engineer is one of the most brilliant, kindest, and well-traveled tour guides in the world of rare teas. Whenever possible, try to use single-origin standard or flavored teas from small purveyors around the world. I use the same philoso-phy for coffee: choose good-quality, fresh beans, use different roasts for different flavor profiles, and buy from local roasters with a great purchasing story that support the coffee belt around the world.

12 Cascara: made from the dried husks of coffee beans, cascara might be a little tough to find in some areas, but local coffee roasters often have a stash to sell. Coffee husks have a stunning fruity character while being very earthy, like the beans. Cascara made from cacao beans is also a great product and can be found online.

Equipment, Tools & Accessories

Every bar requires some basic tools so you can have the confidence to mix like the pros. Below are lists of the items I have in my home and have recommended to my guests or used to stock my professional bars.

Equipment & Tools

Two-piece tin-on-tin cocktail shaker: an industry term to describe a full metal shaker. Whether it's stainless steel, a three-piece cobbler, a mason jar, or a glass-on-metal Boston shaker, we use this equipment to emulsify ingredients together with ice.

Hawthorne strainer: a small strainer with a coil of metal gills, commonly used to strain or hold back the ice and other large particles from a cocktail shaker.

Julep strainer: a strainer similar to a Hawthorne, but without the coil gills that hold back big particles; commonly used to hold back ice in a mixing glass.

Mesh sieve or tea strainer: used when a double-strain or fine-strain method is called for in the recipe. This gives your "up" or "neat" drink with citrus and other ingredients a luxurious finish, free from ice shards from the cocktail shaker.

Mixing glass: used with spirit-forward drinks to chill and dilute simultaneously, using a bar spoon and ice.

Bar spoon: the ubiquitous accompaniment to a mixing glass.

Ice scoop: Crafthouse makes a nice, affordable one that's small, low-profile, and narrow on the sides to ensure the ice you scoop heads into the glass and not all over your counter.

Jigger: this measuring device is one of the most important tools in bartending, as precise measurements ensure that all the ingredients are balanced in the glass, mixing glass, or shaker. Make sure your jigger has measurements written on it, in either imperial or metric.

Silicone ice molds: these make uniform cubes in varying sizes—1-inch (2.5 cm), 3 inches (7.5 cm), etc.—and not only make your finished drinks look great, but also chill and dilute evenly. Ditch the ice trays that came with your freezer and use these instead.

Ice pick and carving tools: if you are keen to make clear blocks of ice and carve cubes, diamonds, or other large pieces for your drinks, these advanced tools will be necessary, along with a serrated knife, a muddler or mallet, and a cooler box.

Lewis bag: fill this burlap bag with ice cubes, close the top, and smash it with a mallet to make crushed ice to order, then use that ice scoop mentioned above. Store it in a sanitary place in the kitchen or the freezer until you need it. Wash it in the washing machine with your tea towels.

Wooden mallet: used as the accompaniment to a Lewis bag.

Muddler: I don't use a muddler often, but when I do, it's to break down citrus peels, flowers, and sugars in oleo saccharums (oil sugars), or fresh fruit or citrus wedges. I don't recommend using muddlers for fresh herbs unless you have a very gentle touch. Often, the muddler does more harm than good with precious mint leaves.

Y-shaped peeler: used to remove just the top layer of the citrus and leave the pith behind.

Paring knife: a small, super-sharp paring knife is all you need.

Chopping board: choose one you can store and sanitize easily, like food-grade plastic, and use it with your paring knife.

Citrus hand press: a variety of sizes are available to juice whatever size of citrus fruit you've got. I recommend purchasing a larger one appropriate for grapefruits and oranges, as the lemons and limes still fit.

Ice tongs and linen napkins: I am twitchy about hands on ice; it's that simple. When no one is watching and you're making drinks for yourself at home, go nuts, but guests at your home or bar want you to exercise cleanliness at all times. Consider placing your ice from the freezer in an ice bowl or bucket and using the tongs to distribute it. A linen napkin folded into a small square is a nice touch with scoops of ice, to help guide the ice into the glass, mixing glass, or cocktail shaker. It's the little things that make a big difference.

Bar towels, an apron, chopsticks for your hair: ensure that your hair is pulled back and that you have bar towels, hand sanitizer, and an apron if you wish. Bartending is just like cooking: you don't want any surprises found in the glass.

Notebook and recipe book: keep track of your results, things you liked, things you didn't, and the inspiration for your creation. This is how all bartenders start out, whether at home or in a professional setting. It's great to keep a diary of interesting drink names and flavor discoveries at the market too.

Accessories

Aromatizer/spray bottle: I love to add aromatics to drinks, and it's a wonderful touch to add them tableside or let your guest do it themselves. You can get 1-ounce (30 mL) bottles with aromatized tops online and store them in the fridge door with your mix. Experiment with the recommended sprays in this book!

Cocktail picks: avoid single-use plastics. Metal or wood picks are great, and there are some fun designs out there to hold your onions, olives, or cherries.

Reusable straws: I have a few different types, like metal spoon straws and bamboo reusable straws, in both wide-mouth for bubble tea, smoothies, and crushed ice tiki drinks, and narrow-mouth for everything else that requires a straw. I generally don't recommend straws unless they're used in the drink specifically. Paper straws are fine in a pinch, but they melt or get floppy quickly if the drink isn't consumed fast enough.

Microplane: used to finely grate coffee beans, nutmeg, cinnamon, and other spices to a powder, perfect for drink toppings.

Coasters: go crazy collecting these! Try stone, metal, cardboard, reusable, recyclable, upcycled, you name it—just stay away from single-use plastics.

Spice shaker: I use this for different drink toppings, like coconut cream or cacao powder, and it's nice to have one on hand.

Glassware & Service Pieces

Old-fashioned/rocks glasses: the common glass for the old fashioned, in 9-ounce (275 mL) and 13-ounce (400 mL) sizes. The 9-ounce (275 mL) is perfect for a neat whiskey sour with egg white, filled to the brim.

Collins/highball glasses: used for long drinks, these range between 9 and 16 ounces (275 and 500 mL). The standard is 12 to 13 ounces (375 to 400 mL).

Nick and Nora glasses: popularized by bartender Dale DeGroff and named for two movie detectives, these are a beautiful alternative to cocktail glasses. Sizes generally range from 6 to 9 ounces (175 to 275 mL). A martini or V-shape glass is okay in a pinch.

Cocktail glasses/coupes/coupettes: these are the ultimate (and likely most popular) cocktail glasses, perfect for everything from martinis to daisies and sours. Sizes range from 5½ to 13 ounces (165 to 400 mL).

Coffee glasses: used for Irish or specialty coffees. You can choose one with a small stem, one with a handle, or a small, tapered tumbler. Sizes range from 6 to 9 ounces (175 to 275 mL).

Teapot, teacups, and saucers: go vintage if you can, with mix-and-match cups and saucers, and have fun. I use these most often for punches, as tea is a common ingredient.

Julep cups: used for crushed ice drinks like the mint julep, these always require a straw.

Punch jugs or bottles: for large-format serving containers, don't automatically grab a bowl and ladle—you can have fun here. Think about items that look beautiful, as well as ones you can transport and store in the fridge.

Tiki mugs: most tiki drinks require a lot of volume, between 13 and 20 ounces (400 and 600 mL) in some cases, so choose interesting cups and pieces that can become collector editions. I like wood and ceramic options.

Mason jars with a lid: if you're on the go, at a picnic, or can't be fussed to get the cocktail shaker and glass, an 8-ounce (250 mL) mason jar is a great vessel to both build the drink and serve it. Use mason jars to store spices or can the flower jellies in this book as well.

Sidecar/carafe: used for the "extra" portion of your drink. Think of a martini or stirred drink that you want to serve in a small chilled glass. With a sidecar, you can pour a small portion into the chilled glass, with a rocks glass filled with crushed ice on the side and the remaining cocktail in the sidecar. What a lovely way to keep your cocktail cold for longer.

French press: used for in-the-moment infusions. Choose one that holds 4 or 8 cups (1 or 2 L). It works nicely to make a punch or sangria, and can be used hot or cold.

General Kitchen Tools

Blender: both drinks and mise en place ingredients benefit from the power of a blender.

Immersion circulator (or sous vide or stem thermometer): used to hold a pot of water at a steady temperature for a period of time while the ingredients cook inside a sealed heatproof food-safe plastic bag. This is one of my preferred methods for infusions and syrups.

Spice mill: a small grinder used just for spices is a good investment; a small coffee grinder works too.

Carbonated drink maker: the best choice for the recipes in this book is the Drinkmate, which can carbonate any liquid. A SodaStream will only carbonate water, but is fine for those recipes where that's all you need to do.

Fermentation jars with an air lock: used for the ferments in the book. You can get one online or at most specialty homebrew stores. I use 2- to 4-quart (2 to 4 L) jars.

Juicer: whether you choose a centrifugal or masticating juicer, it's great to have one on hand. I find the masticating juicers better for tough ingredients like ginger, sweet potatoes, turmeric, beets, and celery.

Smoking box, handheld smoker, and wood chips: Crafthouse makes an amazing apparatus to use with a handheld smoker and wood chips at home. The metal box with glass sides is as beautiful as it is functional, with access doors that open on both ends. The handle on top makes it easy to move around, and the box fits two to three drinks at a time. I use it for cocktails and for smoked olives. In a pinch, you can create your own at home, using a smoking gun, or smoldering spices and wood, with a cloche top or cake dome—I used a large jar for the recipes in this book!

Barbecue lighter: small or large, these are great to have on hand to light the chips for the smoker, as well as to flame orange peel oils over a drink.

Kitchen torch: a kitchen blowtorch is used for heavy-duty toasting of spices or citrus wedges. You can find one online or at a hardware store.

Digital microscale: this is critical for accurately measuring partial grams of certain spices, like cloves and cardamom; powdered acids, like malic, tartaric, and citric; and thickeners, stabilizers, and powders.

Standard digital scale: use this for larger measurements by the gram, and for batches. You'll see in this book that the recipes are often measured by weight. This is the most accurate way to create the mise en place and subrecipes for the book, and ultimately great cocktails. A digital scale is an inexpensive tool that you'll love having in your kitchen and bar. Get one!

Measuring cups and spoons: I like tools that display both imperial and metric measurements, but you can use either system to measure the liquid ingredients in this book. Just be sure to stick with whichever system you choose and use it consistently, so you get the proportions right.

Dehydrator: this is an inexpensive tool that will allow you more flexibility in preserving fruits, vegetables, and other ingredients for garnishes or tea blends.

Thermometer: try to find one that displays both Fahrenheit and Celsius measurements.

Cheesecloth and mesh sieves: I use these in most of my mise en place recipes, and for a smooth and refined product.

Various saucepans with tight-fitting lids.

UNDERSTANDING PROOF & ABV

Each recipe is accompanied with a proof or ABV (alcohol by volume) level. Here's what the terminology means:

Zero Proof/NA = less than 0.5% ABV

I want to ensure that folks reading this book who are looking for great zero-proof drinks can find them. There should be something in here for everyone. The book supports 0.0% cocktails if you have a full alcohol allergy or aversion—just remove the bitters.

Low Proof = between 0.5% and 8% ABV

Some of the ferments, like kombucha, natural ginger beer, and tepache, as well as aromatized wines and highballs, fall into this "everyday" category. It's lovely, easy drinking.

Mid Proof = between 8% and 13% ABV

A drink for unwinding, celebrating, and enjoying that's a bit punchier than low proof.

Standard Proof = over 13% ABV

Spirit-forward drinks fall into this category. All ABVs are calculated with a 25% dilution, more or less, through building, shaking, and stirring with ice.

COCKTAIL DESIGN

Back in 2009 at The Refinery, I started using classic inspirations for my recipe designs to help with staff training and educate the guests as much as possible on the menu; it worked so well that I continued this practice as a consultant for the Four Seasons Hotel Group and beyond. My cocktail designs and flavor combinations could be as creative and "out there" as I wanted (same with their esoteric names), but they were all rooted in a design that everyone could understand. You'll see this philosophy reflected in each recipe.

Regional Inspiration

Each entry in this book is inspired by a place I have visited, a person or people I've met, a formative childhood memory, a moment in time, a story I have shared with friends, or the perfect instant when I was able to stop and smell the roses. I have been awed by the hospitality, warmth, and generosity shared with me on so many occasions when people opened their hearts and homes. Learning about culture and heritages different from my own has affected me deeply, and it's an honor to share these moments with you. Celebrating and appreciating the cultures of the world makes my drinks' aromas brighter, the flavors sharper, and the memories everlasting.

Bartending Basics

There are a few basic rules to follow when you're making drinks, similar to those for cooking.

- Follow the recipe. Make it once, analyze the results, and experiment on your next attempts.
- Don't use dangerous ingredients because you think they're cool. Avoid activated charcoal, tobacco, and raw apricot kernels, to name a few, especially in combination with alcohol.
- Be mindful of allergies to nuts, eggs, seeds, barks, or any other ingredients that may exist in your circle. Always use caution when trying new ingredients, and ask your guests about their allergies and aversions ahead of time. This is how bartenders and cooks operate in professional settings. Get to know your friends a bit better by asking questions about their desert island ingredients and what their top three cocktails are, then build on those ideas.
- The golden ratio of acid to sugar: an equal measure of 1:1 simple syrup to lemon or lime juice—not too sweet, not too sour, nicely balanced. It hits all angles of the palate equally. This is why a daiquiri is so perfect, a Tom Collins or gimlet is sensational, and a whiskey sour is brilliant. To achieve a drier drink, pull back the sugar by ¼ ounce (7.5 mL); for a touch more sweetness, pull back the citrus by the same amount. This is particularly helpful when lemons and limes are more sour than normal, as you'll be able to adjust your drinks easily. The All-Purpose Cordial (page 232) allows you to keep a golden ratio ingredient on hand and ready to use.
- There are recipes for cordials and shrubs throughout the book. Preparation is key when trying a recipe, so ensure all your mise en place ingredients are ready in advance so you can focus on making the cocktail.

- Stirred drinks are generally spirit-based and are gently chilled and diluted simultaneously for a smooth final product. They can be served up (neat) or on the rocks, to your preference or the recipe recommendation. Generally speaking, with a standard stir for thirty rotations, the liquid volume of the cocktail should increase by 25% with dilution. This is balance—water lengthens and softens flavors, allowing all the ingredients to bloom and shine together.

- Shaken drinks are usually a blend of nonalcoholic ingredients with or without spirit bases, hard-shaken with ice to ensure emulsification, chill, and dilution simultaneously. I always tell folks I am teaching to make drinks, "Shake the cocktail like it owes you money!" A hard shake takes practice, and it's ultra-satisfying to do. Generally speaking, with a standard shake for five to seven seconds, the liquid volume of the cocktail should increase by 25% with dilution. Double-straining shaken drinks with a fine-mesh sieve will catch the ice and ingredient particles, leaving the perfectly smooth cocktail to enjoy.

- Chilled glassware, good-quality clear ice, and other flourishes add to the drink's flavor and your experience. Standard ice cubes are great, but make them with filtered water and keep them away from aromatic items in your freezer or your drinks won't taste very good.

Agave Spirits

All-Purpose Flower

I first met Katie Ingram at Dish 'n Dazzle, a fundraising event for the BC Hospitality Foundation, in 2014. She was one of the bartenders showcasing her cocktails, inspired by the flowers and fragrances of Stanley Park. Katie's a performer; she had an awesome way of presenting the information—comedic and energetic. "She's got the right stuff," I thought, and invited her to come interview at Uva Wine & Cocktail Bar, the venue I was running. Katie was an instant fit on the team and quickly became the lead bartender. Uva was cursed with only one cocktail station and ice well to use (we called it "the single occupant cockpit") in a high-volume environment with high-end service, a huge and ever-rotating cocktail list, and opening hours of nineteen per day. The joke became "If you want to learn high-speed, high-volume, high-end cocktails, Uva is your place." But Katie was always destined for bigger things. She moved on from Uva to take over the bar program at L'Abattoir, and was part of the opening team at Elisa steakhouse. Over the years, Katie has become part of the Bittered Sling team as one of our primary ambassadors, a top finalist and winner of numerous competitions, and a brilliant human who sponges up everything she learns. Anything Katie puts her mind to is researched and executed flawlessly. More than that, she is a great friend, incredibly creative, and a kind soul. This drink represents some of the flavors from the first cocktail she ever made me, as well as her adaptable "all-purpose" attitude.

Method

To a shaker filled with cubed ice, add the tequila, vermouth, orange juice, cordial, and bitters. Using some force, shake hard for 10 seconds. Using a small fine-mesh bar sieve to catch the loose ice chips, double strain into a cocktail glass or coupe. For the garnish, attach edible flowers and a fancy orange twist to the glass with a clothes peg.

Serves 1

Area of inspiration: Vancouver, British Columbia
Inspired by: the Margarita

———

1½ ounces (45 mL) blanco tequila

¾ ounce (22.5 mL) Nebula Pink Vermouth (page 238) or Cocchi Rosa vermouth

¾ ounce (22.5 mL) fresh orange juice

¾ ounce (22.5 mL) All-Purpose Flower Cordial (page 46)

1 dash orange bitters
(like Bittered Sling Orange & Juniper)

Garnish: Fresh edible flowers, fancy orange twist

Daiquirita

While rich, aged rums are delicious in many drinks, bartenders always crave the zesty character of white rums in their daiquiris. While in Taipei, in 2017, my husband, Jonathan, ponied up to the bar next to Ueno-san, the owner of Bar High Five in Tokyo. He wanted something special to satisfy his craving for both dark rum and blanco tequila. The Daiquirita is the perfect blend of the daiquiri and margarita. We're always playing with "split spirit bases" as bartenders. It allows you to custom-blend the flavors and textures you're looking for each time. It's not uncommon to blend rums, for example, and is often seen in tiki-style drinks, like the Zombie cocktail. This recipe is lovely and can use any rum and tequila combination you like. However, for the best results, I recommend a rich, oak-matured rum and a 100% blue agave blanco tequila. I'm really hoping this concept catches on and can't wait to see which other classic drinks might benefit from the same split-base idea (I'm thinking the Mercado Mai Tai, page 36; Century Plant, page 42; and Apple-ation, page 50). This way of building flavors gives bartenders the freedom to learn and express themselves through different discovery bottles.

Method

To a shaker filled with cubed ice, add the tequila, rum, lime juice, lemon juice, and simple syrup. Using some force, shake hard for 10 seconds. Using a small fine-mesh bar sieve to catch the loose ice chips, double strain into a Nick and Nora glass or cocktail coupe. Garnish with a thin lime wheel across the top of the drink.

Serves 1

Area of inspiration: Taipei, Taiwan, China
Inspired by: the Daiquiri and the Margarita

——

1 ounce (30 mL) blanco tequila

1 ounce (30 mL) high-quality aged rum

½ ounce (15 mL) fresh lime juice

½ ounce (15 mL) fresh lemon juice

½ ounce (15 mL) Simple Syrup (page 47)

Garnish: Thin lime wheel

Family Affair

Fifty-four years ago, Señora Elmy Bermejo and her husband, Tommy, opened Tommy's Mexican Restaurant in the Richmond District of San Francisco. Today, not only do I have the great pleasure of working closely with their son, Señor Julio Bermejo, and their daughter, Señorita Elmy, but I pay tribute to the entire family on the menu I created at the Four Seasons San Francisco with the It's a Family Affair cocktail. Julio is a legend in our industry—not just in San Francisco—and a brilliant bartender and agave spirits educator. On the outside, the restaurant is deceiving; it looks like a typical family-owned Mexican joint. But switch gears and head to the bar, and it's likely that Julio or one of his incredible bartenders will greet you with a perfectly balanced Tommy's Margarita (which Julio invented, replacing the orange curaçao in the recipe with agave syrup to better connect it to the spirit), an agave spirits tutorial, and a guest versus bartender "fastest hand-juiced limes" contest. Julio's signature whiteboard welcomes special guests by the thousands each year (names changing daily), but the motto never rubs off: "Don't forget how lucky you are to live in San Francisco." The most important thing, beyond cocktails, is the sentiment. Not only does Tommy's have the largest agave spirits collection in the world, but their chosen family in San Francisco and around the globe is an example of the incredible impact possible in the drinks industry: they're building community one drink at a time. We are so lucky to have Tommy's as a beacon of hospitality, love, and flavor in our industry.

Method

To a shaker filled with cubed ice, add the tequila, cordial, bitters, jalapeño, and salt. Using some force, shake hard for 5 seconds. Using a small fine-mesh bar sieve to catch the loose ice chips and jalapeño, double strain into a highball glass. Garnish with the lime wheel and basil leaf.

Serves 1

Area of inspiration: San Francisco, California
Inspired by: the Tommy's Margarita

———

2 ounces (60 mL) blanco tequila

¾ ounce (22.5 mL) Basil Cordial (page 46)

2 dashes spicy aromatic bitters
(like Bittered Sling Moondog Latin)

4 slices green jalapeño pepper
(leave the seeds if you like it spicy)

Pinch sea salt

Garnish: Fresh basil leaf

Gondwana

While I was competing in a huge competition in South Africa, I created roughly forty original cocktails for the program. The Gondwana is one of my favorites. As a history and geography buff, I've always been fascinated by the supercontinent Pangea. During the "Around the World" challenge, I was tasked to make a drink inspired by my home in Canada and the competition's location in South Africa. The rest was up to me. My idea was to split the cocktails in two: one inspired by the top half of the Pangea continent, called Laurasia, and the second by the bottom half, called Gondwana. I took the judges on a journey without a backpack, allowing them to imagine walking across the lands and picking up ingredients along the way to create an inspired, interesting serve, prepared in a different and memorable way. Granted, my fictitious journey was faster and safer than the real thing—we avoided the many volcanoes, large, inquisitive animals, and early humanoid creatures—but the spirit of adventure was there. The Gondwana locations showcased in the cocktail are Mexico, Africa, India, and Australia.

Method

Fill a mixing glass with cubed ice. Add the tequila, vermouth, curaçao, and bitters. Stir with a bar spoon for 15 to 20 rotations. Using a julep strainer, strain into a Nick and Nora glass or cocktail coupe. For the garnish, use a peeler to remove a nice piece of peel from a washed orange. Using a paring knife, trim the edges of the peel on all sides. Twist the peel to express the oil over the cocktail, then drop it into the glass.

Serves 1

Area of inspiration: Southern Hemisphere
Inspired by: the Martinez

———

1½ ounces (45 mL) reposado tequila

¾ ounce (22.5 mL) Red Leather Vermouth (page 238) or red vermouth

½ ounce (15 mL) Cardamom Curaçao (page 46)

2 dashes orange bitters
(like Bittered Sling Orange & Juniper)

Garnish: Orange twist

Mercado Mai Tai

To my mind, there's no better way to see Mexico City than to find a nearby market and taste the variety of produce, spices, and spirits found within. Mexico's regional beverages and cuisines are some of the most diverse in the world: the wine-making regions to the north; the agricultural belt traveling down the Pacific coast; the abundant grain, agave, and seed plantations inland and to the south; and tropical fruit, vegetables, and citrus to the east. To truly celebrate the flavors of Mexico, enjoy this twist on a classic Mai Tai, with a split base of rum and tequila. The blend adds a delicious complexity; melding spirit categories rather than just different rums opens up a new world of flavor. Sometimes bartenders feel like we need permission to blend, so please, go ahead and experiment. In this cocktail, the mole is the focus, in the form of a rich orgeat-style syrup (traditionally made from almonds) that is an obligatory ingredient in a Mai Tai. The result is a wonderfully inspired cocktail with an earthy complexity—and it's nut-free for our friends with a nut allergy. Feel free to use the Pumpkin Seed Orgeat in a traditional Mai Tai too.

Method

Add cubed ice to a Lewis bag and smash into chips with a mallet. Fill a shaker with more cubed ice. Add the tequila, rum, orgeat, lime juice, orange juice, and bitters. Shake for a few seconds to chill. Fill a tiki mug with a combination of cubed and crushed ice. Strain the cocktail over the ice, and add more crushed ice on top. Garnish with flowers, herbs, and fruit. Serve with a long, wide reusable or compostable straw.

Serves 1

Area of inspiration: Mexico City, Mexico
Inspired by: the Mai Tai

———

¾ ounce (22.5 mL) blanco tequila

¾ ounce (22.5 mL) dark rum

¾ ounce (22.5 mL) Pumpkin Seed Orgeat (page 47)

¾ ounce (22.5 mL) fresh lime juice

¾ ounce (22.5 mL) fresh orange juice

2 dashes spicy aromatic bitters
(like Bittered Sling Moondog Latin)

Garnish: Fresh edible flowers, fresh herbs (like mint and basil), fruit

DISCOVERING THE MERCADO

I remember every visit to Mexico City vividly; I am lucky to be so familiar with it. On a recent trip with a group of twenty bartenders from around the Americas, I was strolling through the beautiful Mercado de San Juan. Situated in the middle of the bustling Centro district, this market is one of the most incredible places to buy ingredients. I wanted to shop there for my session, which discussed how to bring classic cocktails to life using local flavors in interesting ways, and the market is so cool that bartenders, chefs, and a film crew decided to come with me. Everyone was interested in my thought process from ingredient to cocktail—where the ideas, stories, and flavors originate. I tried to explain first in English, then in my very limited Spanish. (While the group seemed impressed, the puzzled looks from the food stand keepers said otherwise.)

At a Mexican mercado, you cannot touch any fruit, vegetable, or other ingredient. You must ask the stand's keeper for a taste, and then they hop down from their pyramid of produce (quite literally—each stand is built into a prism, with them at the top), pull out a machete, and begin carving the selected item for you in an effort to secure a purchase if you enjoy the flavor and service. Meanwhile, the dozens of competing stand keepers argue jokingly, trying to lure you and steal business from their neighbors.

My first bites of ripe cherimoya, fresh (unfermented) cacao beans, mangosteen, star fruit, durian, and other fruits grown in Mexico were all delicious. So I ordered a few fruits and paid the keeper, and we carried on. "Wow, have you ever tasted anything like this?" I exclaimed. I couldn't even describe the flavors. "It's like coffee meets pumpkin meets maple syrup," one bartender said about an acorn squash preserved with piloncillo (a type of raw sugar) at the next stand. I was feeling pretty good! My Spanish was vaguely understandable, fruit had been acquired, and the group was inquisitive, like they'd had their eyes opened for the first time.

We approached my favorite part of the market—the mole stand—and the keepers, a group of older women, seemed to remember me. They were sitting, having coffee, waiting for curious shoppers like us to wander over. The warmth of their smiles permeated instantly, reminding me of meeting my grandmother Rose for coffee. Many people are familiar with the chocolate version of mole but don't realize it can be made from a wide range of ingredients. *Mole* simply means "sauce." The mole I wanted my group to taste was made with pumpkin seeds and spices—a combination I had purchased from these women on an earlier trip. Countless little taster spoons flooded the crowd as they sampled different moles— cashew, peanut, chocolate, sesame, you name it—all delicious, all homemade, and all stored in 5-gallon (20 L) pails, including a few disguised as a table, where the ladies played cards.

I wanted 200 grams (about ½ pound) of the pumpkin seed mole for a recipe I would make later that day. Feeling overly confident, I said, "*Señora, por favor, dos mil gramos de mole de calabaza.*" They stared at me sweetly as their smiles widened. I paid the bill and out came a *bucket* of mole. Instead of 200 grams, I had ordered 2 kilograms—a face-palm moment for me. "*Gracias!*" they yelled.

Yonge Street

One of my coolest memories from my childhood in Toronto is feeling like my brothers and I "owned" Yonge Street. Our afternoons were spent chasing comic books (my dad, Michael, had a collection of 40,000) and eating ice cream floats. The evenings were all about movies, on film and television—old movies, new movies (including premieres of various 1980s favorites at the Uptown), classics, and director's cuts. Some were incredible, while others were so terrifying they became a "checkbox" later in life (been there done that) and a haunting reminder of why I still can't watch horror films. We were encouraged to make our own movies, complete with masks, costumes, and fantastical situations, which brought out our inner entertainers even more. "Kid Video," as the handwritten label on the side of the Betamax tape in my dad's video collection called it, was a combination of our greatest moments: our live news program, called *The World Today*, featuring me as the main anchor and my brother Jake as the sportscaster, named Roger; Milli Vanilli lip-synching videos; and *The Monsters of Forest Hill*, which starred Jake and Sasha in monster costumes. When I created a cocktail inspired by those moments, Yonge Street seemed an appropriate name—the location that started it all. The tequila represents my mother's drink of choice; the blue curaçao, the color of my favorite teams: the Toronto Blue Jays and Maple Leafs. The lime is the counterbalance to our family's "chili pepper roulette" games. The juice signifies our breakfasts together. The orgeat symbolizes my mother's vegetarian lifestyle—almonds gave her the power to persevere and walk everywhere. And the bitters provide the nostalgic flavor of root beer, which takes me right back to monster truck shows at the SkyDome and concession orders at the opening night of the Teenage Mutant Ninja Turtles movies. I thank my dad, for so many of these memories and, of course, the coasters are his.

Serves 1

Area of inspiration: Toronto, Ontario
Inspired by: the Margarita

———

1 ounce (30 mL) blanco tequila

½ ounce (15 mL) blue curaçao liqueur

¾ ounce (22.5 mL) Orgeat (page 47) or store-bought orgeat syrup

¾ ounce (22.5 mL) fresh lime juice

¾ ounce (22.5 mL) fresh pineapple juice

2 dashes aromatic bitters
(like Bittered Sling Plum & Rootbeer)

Garnish: Thin slice dehydrated or fresh pineapple, pineapple fronds

Method

To a shaker filled with cubed ice, add the tequila, curaçao, orgeat, lime juice, pineapple juice, and bitters. Using some force, shake hard for 5 seconds. Using a small fine-mesh bar sieve to catch the loose ice chips, double strain into a highball glass. Garnish with the pineapple slice and fronds.

Century Plant

I always try to see something different each time I visit Mexico City. On one trip, I was delighted to spend the day with my friend Fernando Camacho, who hired a taxi to take us to Teotihuacan (the "City of Gods"). The city was (and is!) a marvel for its time (100 CE), with pyramids and many small neighborhoods, roads, and smaller structures. The Pyramid of the Sun, rising along the Avenue of the Dead between the Pyramid of the Moon and the Citadel (a sunken square in the center of Teotihuacan), is the largest structure in Teotihuacan and one of the largest in Mesoamerica. We climbed the pyramid, and perhaps it was the moment or the energy or a coincidence, but the overcast sky parted ever so slightly above our heads to allow brilliant sunshine to hit the tip of the pyramid. I believe in the energy of people, the power of community, and the small nuggets of hope that keep us together, and this beautiful day was a reminder of that. It's strange to think this city was here long before us and will be here long after us. After we descended, we walked several miles, with the pyramid looming in the distance. We rewarded ourselves with a roadside taco feast paired with micheladas. This drink is an evolution of that wonderful day.

Method

To a shaker filled with cubed ice, add the mezcal, cordial, aloe vera juice, and salt. Using some force, shake hard for 5 seconds. Using a Hawthorne strainer, strain into a Collins glass filled with cubed ice. Top with equal parts ginger beer and beer. Garnish with the lime wheel and parsley.

Serves 1

Area of inspiration: Teotihuacan, Mexico
Inspired by: the Michelada

———

1 ounce (30 mL) mezcal

1 ounce (30 mL) Celery Cordial (page 47)

1 ounce (30 mL) aloe vera juice

Pinch kosher salt

Sparkling ginger beer (nonalcoholic), cold

Saison beer (6.0% or nonalcoholic), cold

Garnish: Lime wheel (fresh or dehydrated), fresh parsley sprig

Instant Crush

On a humid April day in 2013, we touched down in Buenos Aires, Argentina. Both Jonathan and I were excited to be there; our little brand from Canada, Bittered Sling, had been invited to be part of Tales of the Cocktail on Tour, a product and educational showcase for bartenders in Latin America. We were to bring a taste of Canada and provide some unique specialty cocktail bitters, developed by a chef and bartender team, for the bartenders to learn and use. Argentina didn't carry many specialized cocktail modifiers at the time. Bartenders were innovative DIY-ers making their own yerba mate cups, metal straws, bitters, vermouths, you name it. We were so thrilled to be involved, but had met with an unlucky incident in Vancouver: our flight to Toronto was delayed by three hours, as the plane was broken. Equally uneasy about the "broken plane" and the potential of missing our connection, we panicked, worried about what else might go wrong. We called a supplier in Toronto and asked them to ship three bottles of each Bittered Sling flavor to our airport hotel in Toronto, just in case there were any problems with the shipment we'd sent to Argentina. Little did we know that Bittered Sling's journey to South America would be complicated by outrageous customs issues, missing cargo, extortion, and in the end no bitters! What had started as a thrilling moment—a milestone in Bittered Sling's short life—created major anxiety and turned into a truly sad development to share with the Tales team. Thank goodness we had the samples in our luggage to save the day. Bartenders from across Latin America joined us, and we were over the moon to get the seal of approval from this amazing crew, particularly Pablo Carrizo (an awesome bartender who now lives in Colombia). He loved our bitters. More importantly, he cared about our story and really cared about us. Pablo and the rest of the group were happy we'd made the journey, giving a spotlight to Latin American bartenders, sharing our knowledge, supporting their bars, and spending quality time together. Pablo and I have stayed in close touch and have worked on many projects together, and it's his attitude beyond the bottle that makes him, and so many other bartenders, special.

This imaginative cocktail is inspired by Argentina's love for fernet, a bitter, digestive, relatively dry liqueur known as the "bartender's handshake" around the world. We created it to remember our challenging yet emotional trip to Argentina, where we shook hands and made friends for life, and it's an amalgamation of Jonathan's favorite ingredients in one drink.

Method

Fill a mixing glass with cubed ice. Add the mezcal, tequila, vermouth, crème de cassis, fernet, and bitters. Stir with a bar spoon for 15 to 20 rotations. Using a julep strainer, strain into an old-fashioned glass filled with cubed ice. For the garnish, use a peeler to remove a nice piece of peel from a washed orange. Using a paring knife, trim the edges of the peel on all sides. Twist the peel to express the oil over the cocktail, then drop it into the glass.

Serves 1

Area of inspiration: Buenos Aires, Argentina
Inspired by: the Vieux Carré

———

½ ounce (15 mL) mezcal

1½ ounces (45 mL) blanco tequila

¾ ounce (22.5 mL) Starlight White Vermouth (page 239) or white vermouth

¼ ounce (7.5 mL) crème de cassis

1 bar spoon Fernet-Branca

2 dashes spicy aromatic bitters
(like Bittered Sling Moondog Latin)

Garnish: Orange twist

Mise en Place Recipes

Basil Cordial

Makes 16 ounces (500 mL)

25 grams fresh basil leaves and stems

300 grams superfine or granulated sugar

15 grams citric acid

10 ounces (300 mL) filtered water

Wash the basil leaves and stems and pat dry with a clean towel. To a blender, add the basil, sugar, citric acid, and water. Blend on medium until the sugar is dissolved. Strain the liquid through a mesh sieve to catch the large pieces, then through cheesecloth to microfilter. This syrup should be vibrant and green. Store in a sanitized bottle, labeled with the date, in the fridge for up to 10 days.

———

Cardamom Curaçao

Makes 8 ounces (250 mL), 35% ABV

3 whole green cardamom pods

1 whole black cardamom pod

8 ounces (250 mL) orange curaçao or Triple Sec liqueur

Add all ingredients to a small jar, close the lid, and shake. Infuse for 24 hours. Strain the liquid through a mesh sieve into a sanitized bottle and label with the date and ABV. Store indefinitely with your other room-temperature alcohols.

All-Purpose Flower Cordial

Makes 16 ounces (500 mL)

200 grams superfine or granulated sugar

70 grams fresh edible flowers

50 grams creamed raw white honey

10.5 grams potato starch

3.5 grams malic acid

3.5 grams citric acid

8 ounces (250 mL) cold filtered water

Add the sugar and flowers to an airtight container, press with a muddler, and close the container. Let stand for 24 hours. The next day, add the honey, potato starch, acids, and water. Stir to dissolve. Strain the liquid through a mesh sieve into a sanitized bottle, label with the date, and store in the fridge for up to 10 days.

Celery Cordial

Makes 16 ounces (500 mL)

4 large celery stalks

10 grams citric acid, divided

200 grams superfine or granulated sugar

Set up a juicer. Chop the celery into small pieces. Add 2 grams of the citric acid to the bottom of a small pitcher and use that to catch the juice. (This prevents the juice from browning.) Run the celery pieces through the juicer. You should have about 7 ounces (200 mL) juice. Stir to dissolve the acids, then strain into a blender. Add the remaining citric acid and sugar. Blend on medium until the sugar is dissolved. Strain the liquid through cheesecloth to microfilter. This syrup should be vibrant and green. Store in a sanitized bottle, labeled with the date, in the fridge for up to 10 days.

———

Orgeat

Makes 16 ounces (500 mL)

500 grams chopped skinless almonds

16 ounces (500 mL) filtered water

500 grams superfine or granulated sugar

Pinch kosher salt

½ ounce (15 mL) white rum

1 drop orange flower water

Add the almonds and water to a nonreactive container, cover, and refrigerate for 24 hours. The next day, transfer the mixture to a blender, along with the sugar, salt, rum, and orange flower water. Blend on medium until the sugar is dissolved. Strain the liquid through cheesecloth and wring out the cheesecloth. (Reserve the nut mixture for another use if you wish.) Store in a sanitized bottle, labeled with the date, in the fridge for up to 10 days.

Pumpkin Seed Orgeat

Makes 16 ounces (500 mL)

500 grams chopped salted white pumpkin seeds

16 ounces (500 mL) filtered water

500 grams superfine or granulated sugar

½ ounce (15 mL) white rum

1 drop orange flower water

Add the seeds and water to a nonreactive container, cover, and refrigerate for 24 hours. The next day, transfer the mixture to a blender, along with the sugar, rum, and orange flower water. Blend on medium until the sugar is dissolved. Strain the liquid through cheesecloth and wring out the cheesecloth. (Reserve the seed mixture for another use if you wish.) Store in a sanitized bottle, labeled with the date, in the fridge for up to 10 days.

———

Simple Syrup

Makes 10 ounces (300 mL)

250 grams superfine or granulated sugar

8 ounces (250 mL) cold filtered water

Add the sugar and the water to a nonreactive container and whisk until the sugar is dissolved. Store in a sanitized bottle, labeled with the date, in the fridge for up to 10 days.

Brandy

Apple-ation

After a long journey from Vancouver to County Cork in the south of Ireland, Jonathan and I were energized, caffeinated, jet-lagged, and hungry. Tucked in the spacious back seat of an eight-passenger van assigned to us by our hosts, we whipped around tight bends, capturing breathtaking vistas one after the other—stunning emerald fields, rolling hills, happy goats and sheep. The chalky white cliffs contrasted with the sea shorelines below. We stopped in a quaint village and stepped out for a stretch and a drink. The first shop we wandered into had what seemed like more whiskey and spirits than the whole of Heathrow Airport (okay, perhaps an exaggeration, but it was a lot of bottles). In the shop, other than the Irish whiskies of course, was a particular spirit that caught my attention: Calvados, an apple- or pear-flavored blended spirit from northern France, aged like cognac in oak barrels. It's funky, delicious, and totally underappreciated, in my opinion. I asked the shopkeeper why it was there, among all the fine whiskies. He responded, "Because apples and whiskey are wonderful together, and those who love our whiskey love other oak-matured spirits from different regions." It was such an intelligent answer, and also what I'd hoped to hear. After a tour of the Midleton Distillery, and a very obscure photo shoot in a barley field, I was inspired to tie the whole experience together—a celebration of these two spirits. The result is the Apple-ation old fashioned, an ode to Ireland.

Method

Fill a mixing glass with cubed ice. Add the Calvados, whiskey, syrup, and both bitters. Place a large ice cube in an old-fashioned glass and, using a julep strainer, strain the cocktail overtop. For the garnish, use a peeler to remove a nice piece of peel from a washed orange. Using a paring knife, trim the edges of the peel on all sides. Twist the peel to express the oil over the cocktail, then drop it into the glass.

Serves 1

Area of inspiration: County Cork, Ireland
Inspired by: the Widow's Kiss and the Old Fashioned

———

1 ounce (30 mL) Calvados apple brandy

1 ounce (30 mL) Irish whiskey

¼ ounce (7.5 mL) Irish gorse syrup (or flower honey)

1 dash celery bitters (like Bittered Sling Cascade Celery)

1 dash cherry bitters (like Bittered Sling Suius Cherry)

Garnish: Orange twist

Liberation

Three of my grandparents served during the Second World War. I know I'm lucky they came home. My grandfather Bryan Mote was a mechanic and spent most of his time in the UK Land Army, while my grandmother Florence Osborn was a Morse code operator in the Women's Royal Air Force (WRAF). On the paternal side, my grandfather Mack Dolgy served in the Royal Canadian Air Force, while my grandmother, Rose Grafstein, played a crucial role on the home front. Their stories played a significant role in our conversations throughout my life, and I was fortunate enough to have them around well into their late eighties and nineties, with Rose still going strong at 103! In 2016, on a work trip to France called "Le Grand Sling," I spent time with seventeen other bartenders in several different areas, including Reims, Epernay, Paris, and Cognac. I have always loved French culture—a joie de vivre and romance built into lived experiences. At every turn, a different plaque illustrating a new story of liberation from occupation emerged. During those times, I thought of my grandparents and read each plaque with a moment of silence and gratitude, sometimes followed by tears. I created this cocktail as a constant reminder to be grateful for every day, as we never know what's around the corner. The drink is yellow and signifies optimism. May the strength, compassion, and love of all those who've served and the families who've supported them live on forever. The map in the photo is an original document from 1938, showing the armed forces' advance across Europe prior to the Second World War. I found it in an antiques shop in Cheltenham, England back in 2003— I've always collected war relics.

Serves 1

Area of inspiration: Champagne, France
Inspired by: the Boulevardier

---

1 ounce (30 mL) Calvados apple brandy

1 ounce (30 mL) Starlight White Vermouth (page 239) or white vermouth

1 ounce (30 mL) white bitter liqueur (like Suze or Luxardo)

2 dashes celery bitters (like Bittered Sling Cascade Celery)

Garnish: Lemon twist

Method

Fill a mixing glass with cubed ice. Add the Calvados, vermouth, liqueur, and bitters. Stir with a bar spoon for 15 to 20 rotations. Using a julep strainer, strain into a rocks glass filled with cubed ice. For the garnish, use a peeler to remove a nice piece of peel from a washed lemon. Using a paring knife, trim the edges on all sides. Twist the peel to express the oil over the cocktail, then drop it into the glass.

Vieux Boréal

Andrea Carlson opened her restaurant Burdock & Co in Vancouver's Mount Pleasant neighborhood in May 2013. Andrea is one of my favorite chefs on the planet and one of the leaders in the farm, buy, eat local movement in Vancouver. While many chefs now champion local, seasonal, and regional, Andrea was one of the pioneers. She has always connected the wild environment, the purveyors, and the dining room in a way that feels effortless. Burdock & Co showcases the convergence of the wild, from deltas to islands, seaside, farms, and coastline, exemplified in a humble, colorful, and delicious expression of the seasons. Working with Andrea and her team on their opening cocktail list rotations was a dream come true and a thrilling project to witness from concept to creation. The Vieux Canadien, or the Vieux Boréal, helped bring the flavors, ethos, and necessity of restaurant cocktail programs into her orbit, using western Canadian ingredients. Andrea changed the game forever in the Vancouver dining scene, paving the way for many women in the industry to rise up and shine the spotlight on their talents.

Method

Fill a mixing glass with cubed ice. Add the brandy, whisky, vermouth, cordial, and bitters. Stir with a bar spoon for 15 to 20 rotations. Using a julep strainer, strain into an old-fashioned glass filled with cubed ice. Thread the brandied cherry onto a cocktail pick and place it in the glass.

Serves 1

Area of inspiration: Northern Canada
Inspired by: the Vieux Carré

———

1 ounce (30 mL) apple brandy
(like Canados by Okanagan Spirits)

1 ounce (30 mL) Canadian single-malt whisky
(like Laird of Fintry by Okanagan Spirits)

¾ ounce (22.5 mL) Infrared Red Vermouth
(page 238) or red vermouth

½ ounce (15 mL) Boréal Cordial (page 66)

2 dashes cherry bitters
(like Bittered Sling Suius Cherry)

Garnish: Brandied cherry

Donostia Askatuta

If you've ever visited San Sebastián, also known as Donostia, in the Basque region of Spain, you've encountered the overwhelming crowds jammed four people deep into the classic tapas bars. Spent toothpicks and crumpled paprika-stained napkins line the floor, brushing your ankles, and cider jets from bottles and casks into ridiculously small glasses, rain or shine. While tourists and food lovers are racing for reservations, we felt compelled to eat like the locals—cooking in our flat, hitting some of the smaller restaurants, and saving our one Michelin experience for a special occasion. In the October morning light, rain fell as the sun peeked through the clouds. Surfers hit the water early as we walked past, our cloth bags filled with fresh pine mushrooms, vegetables from the market, eggs, cheese, and Basque cider. On our way back, Jonathan noticed La Viña tucked on a side street; it was on his list as the place to try the ethereal Basque cheesecake. We walked in, and the overwhelming aroma of freshly baked Basque cheesecakes, with that lovely burnt top, filled the air. We each had a giant piece, alongside a double espresso. Eladio Rivera and Carmen Jiménez opened the restaurant in 1959, focusing on local flavors and hospitality. Today their son, Santiago Rivera, is the chef. For more than seventy years, the restaurant has carried on cooking and baking the traditional Basque favorites that people from all over the world flock to discover. The Donostia Askatuta (Donostia Shaken) is a great drink inspired by that fantastic experience in San Sebastián.

Method

To a shaker, add the brandy, sherry, tea, syrup, bitters, and egg white. Dry shake (without ice) for 5 seconds. Open the shaker and add cubed ice. Tightly close the shaker, and shake again (this allows the egg white to emulsify with the other ingredients and get frothy). Using a small fine-mesh bar sieve to catch the loose ice chips, double strain into a cocktail glass or coupe. Garnish with a dried apple slice across the top of the drink.

Serves 1

Area of inspiration: San Sebastián, Spain
Inspired by: the Espresso Martini

———

¾ ounce (22.5 mL) Spanish brandy

¾ ounce (22.5 mL) amontillado sherry

2 ounces (60 mL) brewed black tea, cool

¾ ounce (22.5 mL) Apple Syrup (page 66)

2 dashes peach bitters
(like Bittered Sling Clingstone Peach)

1 egg white (see note)

Garnish: Dried apple slice

Note: If you are concerned about the food safety of raw eggs, use 1 ounce (30 mL) pasteurized liquid egg whites in place of the egg white.

Good Vibes Only

My friend Javier Santos, Jonathan, and I hosted a group of Canadian bartenders at the Château de Bourg-Charente in Cognac, France. Inside, the grand rooms and salons stretched farther than most apartments, each with their own history and energy. Wine and music flowed, and it was my birthday, April 21. As a six-liter bottle of Pineau des Charentes emerged, things switched gear—a limbo, blindfolds, cheese, cognac, and more cigars than the local market had for sale. A splash of Pineau was poured for each successful limbo (balancing a six-liter bottle over someone's mouth without spilling is very challenging). Our host, the distiller for Marnier-Lapostolle (Grand Marnier) asked us to follow him downstairs. We traveled down the staircase to the basement, the air changed, and we were welcomed into a large cellar with barrels stacked against the walls. It was the room we had heard about, where only the oldest and rarest cognacs were kept. Quietly, a bottle was pulled: a 1930 cognac saved especially for this occasion. Later that evening, as the guests left and six of us remained to stay the night, the 400-year-old château started to speak. Multiple sightings of a small, wispy woman walking the halls were reported, including one where she tried to get the attention of two guests sleeping in the cigar room by bursting from one of their chests like an apparition from the movie *Alien*. The following morning, the staff confirmed that this woman walks through the castle's halls late at night—we even have photo evidence that makes the hairs on my neck stand up to this day. Luckily, we all survived—she's a nice lady who likes company. The cocktail inspired by this experience is perfect for the apéritif hour.

Serves 6

Area of inspiration: Château de Bourg-Charente, France
Inspired by: the French Connection

————

9 ounces (275 mL) cognac

3 ounces (90 mL) Pineau des Charentes fortified wine

1 ounce (30 mL) amaretto liqueur

12 dashes peach bitters
(like Bittered Sling Clingstone Peach)

Garnish: Orange twist

Method

Fill a mixing glass with cubed ice. Add the cognac, Pineau des Charentes, amaretto, and bitters. Pour the chilled and diluted cocktail into a clean bottle with cap, and store in the fridge. To serve, pour 2 ounces (60 mL) per portion and keep the bottle on ice. For the garnish, use a peeler to remove a nice piece of peel from a washed orange. Using a paring knife, trim the edges on all sides. Twist the peel to express the oil over the cocktail, then drop it into the glass.

Jugo de Selva

When I traveled across five countries in South America on the same trip, I saw unique flora and fauna in the Amazon rain forest, the Andes, and the roads leading to and from these vibrant areas. At ámaZ Restaurante in Lima, Peru, bartender Omar Ludwig took us on a memorable journey of the cacao pod. We were familiar with the pods, but Omar scooped the white, gooey pulp (called mucilage) from the membrane into a cheesecloth bag and hung it for several hours under the weight of its own mass. The result was a cacao pulp liquid that can be used as a rich addition to cocktails or fermented to make cacao-type pulque (pulque is a fermented agave nectar beverage that is popular in Mexico) or fermented and distilled to make a vodka-like cacao pulp distillate. That evening, around the dinner table, my colleague Paulo Figueiredo ordered some "Amazonian juices" to try. Each of us had drastically different experiences depending on which juice we chose. Two of us (me and a colleague) fell asleep at the table within ten minutes, and two (Jonathan and our friend Sebas) were acutely aware and almost hyper, ordering the entire menu and wine list—dishes to feed an army—all while speaking rapidly. Paulo himself went on a lucid psychedelic journey, touching his face, cutlery, glassware, tablecloths, upholstery. Call it the power of the Amazon. The fruits are unique to the jungle, have healing properties used by Indigenous tribes, and contribute to making regionally inspired cocktails. While we don't have access to them outside the region, the Jugo de Selva (Jungle Juice) touches back on our "total body experience" that night in Lima.

Method

To a metal tin filled with crushed ice, add the pisco, wine, lime juice, grapefruit juice, coconut water, syrup, and bitters. Using a milkshake machine or a metal bar spoon, agitate for 15 seconds to dilute and chill. Pour into a tiki cup and garnish with the pineapple wedge, mint, flower, and pineapple fronds. Serve with a long, wide reusable or compostable straw.

Serves 1

Area of inspiration: Lima, Peru
Inspired by: the Borgoña Sangria

1 ounce (30 mL) Peruvian pisco

2 ounces (60 mL) good-quality Pinot Noir table wine

1 ounce (30 mL) fresh lime juice

1 ounce (30 mL) fresh grapefruit juice

1 ounce (30 mL) coconut water

1 ounce (30 mL) Lavender Syrup (page 67)

2 dashes peach bitters
(like Bittered Sling Clingstone Peach)

Garnish: Pineapple wedge, fresh mint, edible flower, pineapple fronds

Miraflores Chicha Morada

In 2015, I met a bartender from Lima, Peru, named Joel Chirinos. I was sad that I didn't speak much Spanish and Joel didn't speak much English—it was one of those challenging moments when you're using Google Translate back and forth or just communicating through smiles and gestures. Over the years, Joel and I have kept in touch, and we managed to be in Madrid at the same time a few years ago. I took Joel and his wife, Sofia, out for brunch, and we spent the afternoon walking through the streets. When I went to Lima, Joel was an incredible host. He took Jonathan and me for dinner, and we even spent a day with him and his brilliant daughter, Maria Alessandra, touring his favorite areas of the city, including the Inka Market and the Parque de Los Niños in Miraflores. Peruvian bartenders work with their colleagues around the world to enhance their interpretation of local traditions and flavors. The result is always exceptional and one-of-a-kind. Over the five days Jonathan and I were in Lima, we ate beautiful foods and experienced thoughtful menus and stories shared by local chefs. Some of the flavors will inspire me for years to come. Chicha morada is an extraordinarily delicious purple corn beverage, and Joel was kind enough to share his family's recipe (page 67). He explained, "Since I can remember, it was consumed at home for a celebration. It is our typical punch in Peru, but currently it has become the perfect companion for Criolla food." I have adapted it slightly from Joel's version, but the magic in the recipe continues to inspire me each time I taste it.

Serves 1

Area of inspiration: Lima, Peru
Inspired by: the Cuba Libre

___

¾ ounce (22.5 mL) Peruvian pisco (optional)

¾ ounce (22.5 mL) dry vermouth (optional)

6 ounces (175 mL) Chicha Morada Mix (page 67)

2 dashes aromatic bitters
(like Bittered Sling Plum & Rootbeer)

Garnish: Pineapple wedge, fresh mint

Method

Add ice to one shaker and the pisco, vermouth, chicha morada mix, and bitters to another. Using a loose Hawthorne strainer (one that sits inside the shaker, not on top) to hold the ice back, move the liquid back and forth between the shakers. As you get good at this technique, you'll add a bit more height and aeration. Do this for 10 to 15 seconds, until the liquid is chilled without being overly emulsified or diluted. Strain into a highball glass filled with cubed ice. Garnish with the pineapple wedge.

Note: You can choose to make this zero proof by omitting the pisco and vermouth.

Pasteis de Nata

A food trip to Portugal, especially for a first-timer, is never complete without fresh ceviche, piri-piri chicken, and pasteis de nata (egg tarts). One summer, Jonathan and I spent three weeks in Portugal, Spain, and Morocco with our friends Luca and Kristine. In the Chiado neighborhood of Lisbon where we were staying, it was a scorching 114°F (46°C) and was so humid it felt like we were swimming in a hot tub. Nevertheless, dressed in our lightest linens, we headed out for coffee and walked to the pier. We picked up an incredible pastry and vanilla aroma and, like Froot Loops' Toucan Sam, we followed our noses down the street. We passed famed tram lines, recognizable from every Lisbon postcard, graffiti, blue-and-white-tiled walls, and locals in the midst of their morning routines as the smell grew stronger. Around the corner, a bakery selling only pasteis de nata emerged; the eggy, sweet custard tarts' vanilla scent hung in the air. The flaky pastry was cooked just right, with a golden touch of brown across the pie and a luscious egg filling. Moments like this are unforgettable when you travel, especially when you can capture the flavors in a drink to enjoy down the road.

Method

To a shaker filled with cubed ice, add the cognac, whisky, sherry, syrup, lemon juice, bitters, and the whole egg. Using some force, shake hard for 5 seconds. Using a small fine-mesh bar sieve to catch the loose ice chips, double strain back into the shaker. Tightly close the shaker and shake again (this allows the egg to emulsify with the other ingredients and get frothy). Pour into a specialty coffee glass or teacup and garnish with nutmeg.

Serves 1

Area of inspiration: Lisbon, Portugal
Inspired by: the Egg Flip

———

1 ounce (30 mL) cognac

1 ounce (30 mL) blended scotch whisky

½ ounce (15 mL) fino sherry

¾ ounce (22.5 mL) Toasted Coconut Syrup (page 67)

¾ ounce (22.5 mL) fresh lemon juice

1 dash chocolate bitters
(like Bittered Sling Malagasy Chocolate)

1 egg (see note)

Garnish: Freshly grated nutmeg

Note: If you are concerned about the food safety of raw eggs, use 2 ounces (60 mL) pasteurized liquid whole eggs in place of the egg.

Mise en Place Recipes

Apple Syrup

Makes 16 ounces (500 mL)

4 red or green apples, refrigerated before use

1.5 grams citric acid

1.5 grams tartaric acid

300 grams superfine or granulated sugar

Set up a juicer. Core and chop the apples (with skins) into small pieces. Add the citric and tartaric acids to the bottom of a small pitcher and use that to catch the juice. (This prevents the juice from browning.) Run the apple pieces through the juicer. Stir the juice to dissolve the acids, then strain into a blender and add the sugar. Blend on medium until the sugar is dissolved. Strain the liquid through cheesecloth to microfilter. This syrup should be vibrant. Store in a sanitized bottle, labeled with the date, in the fridge for up to 10 days.

Note: Apples oxidize more slowly if they've been in the fridge.

Boréal Cordial

Makes 16 ounces (500 mL), 24% ABV

1 whole star anise pod

3 grams allspice berries

1 gram whole Szechuan peppercorns

1 gram whole black peppercorns

1 gram whole black cardamom pods

1 gram whole green cardamom pods

1 gram whole green alder cones (optional)

1 gram myrica gale leaves (optional)

1 gram caraway seeds

1 gram cubeb berries

1 gram whole mace blades

11 ounces (350 mL) Calvados apple brandy

5 ounces (150 mL) high-quality maple syrup

Add all ingredients except the maple syrup to a small jar, close the lid, and shake. Infuse for 96 hours (4 days). Strain the liquid and mix in the maple syrup. Pour into a sanitized bottle and label with the date and ABV. Store indefinitely with your other room-temperature alcohols.

Chicha Morada Mix

Makes 1½ quarts (1.5 L)

500 grams dried blue or purple corn

5 whole cloves

2 cinnamon sticks

2 whole star anise pods

300 grams quince, chopped

200 grams green apple, chopped

200 grams pineapple peels

3 quarts (3 L) cold filtered water

2 ounces (60 mL) Simple Syrup (page 47), or to taste

Using a cleaver, cut the blue corn into 1-inch (2.5 cm) thick circles. Add all ingredients except the syrup to a large pot and make sure the water covers everything completely. Bring to a boil, then reduce the heat to low. Cook for 2 hours, stirring occasionally. Remove from the heat and let cool in the pot. Strain with a mesh sieve to catch the large pieces. Repeat if necessary. Transfer the liquid to a large sanitized food-safe container and stir in the syrup. (This is not supposed to be sweet; add just enough sweetener to balance the mix.) Cover, label with the date, and store in the fridge for up to 10 days. Shake or stir before using.

Note: Joel Chirinos tells me that corn's real flavor is in the center, not the kernels, as most people think.

Lavender Syrup

Makes 16 ounces (500 mL)

300 grams superfine or granulated sugar

10 ounces (300 mL) filtered water

2 grams dried food-grade blue lavender flowers

In a small saucepan, combine the sugar and water. Bring to a slow simmer over medium heat, then immediately remove from the heat. (You don't want it to boil; this is just to dissolve the sugar.) In a heatproof container, using a mallet or muddler, smash the lavender until the essential oils and blue powder release. Pour the sugar water over the flowers, but do not stir; let them infuse their flavor without disrupting the pigment release. After 2 minutes, strain the liquid through a fine-mesh sieve into a sanitized bottle. Label with the date and store in the fridge for up to 7 days.

———

Toasted Coconut Syrup

Makes 16 ounces (500 mL)

300 grams superfine or granulated sugar

10 ounces (300 mL) filtered water

100 grams unsweetened coconut flakes

In a bowl, combine the sugar and water, whisking until the sugar is dissolved. Add the coconut to a dry medium saucepan over low heat and stir until golden brown. Add the coconut to the sugar water, cover, and infuse for 30 minutes. Strain the liquid into a sanitized bottle, label with the date, and store in the fridge for up to 10 days.

Gin

Autumn & Eve

The idea of pumpkin spice is funny—especially to cooks like Jonathan. Bartender friends of mine all over the world have strong feelings for and against pumpkin spice. I suppose my feeling on the matter is that orange coloring and spice doesn't cut it, but if you do something truly special with pumpkins or squash, you've earned the right to jump on the annual media bandwagon. So that's where we're going. The Autumn & Eve tries to channel happy Halloween memories spent trick-or-treating as well. I choose to make, serve, and drink it while in full makeup, dressed as a zombie from Candyland (I'm not sure zombies were in that game, but let's reinvent it), and I suggest you do the same. There just better be actual pumpkin in your pumpkin spice—and did I mention that this piña colada riff uses gin instead of rum? Fun.

Method

To a shaker filled with cubed ice, add the gin, sherry, pineapple juice, syrup, lime juice, ice cream, and bitters. Using some force, shake hard for 5 seconds. Using a Hawthorne strainer, strain into a short, thin highball glass. Garnish with cinnamon.

Serves 1

Area of inspiration: Toronto, Ontario
Inspired by: the Piña Colada

———

1 ounce (30 mL) gin

¾ ounce (22.5 mL) fino sherry

1½ ounces (45 mL) fresh pineapple juice

¾ ounce (22.5 mL) Tula Gingerbread Syrup (page 95)

½ ounce (15 mL) fresh lime juice

1 scoop (45 mL) Pumpkin Spice Ice Cream (page 94)

2 dashes chocolate bitters
(like Bittered Sling Malagasy Chocolate)

Garnish: Grated cinnamon

Electric Avenue

I landed in Beirut at three in the afternoon, having spent a week in Berlin training bartenders. The program we had set up in Lebanon, with the help of our local MTV personality, Sarah Salibi, would be fast and furious. I was no stranger to the forty-eight-hour trip to the farthest reaches of the world—it was part of the charm. I had always wanted to visit Beirut, between Dale DeGroff telling me over the years about the "Paris of the Middle East" and hearing stories from Charles Joly as he tried to uncover his family heritage. And now I was there; I couldn't believe it. Sarah picked me up at the hotel, and our first stop was to meet the rest of the team at the office. Everyone was so proud to welcome me to their country and eager to make my trip memorable. On our way up the mountain to the location of our big bartender training session, we stopped at a local shop specializing in flatbreads with za'atar to enjoy on the road. The aroma of spices roasting in an open forno filled the air, and I was in heaven.

Throughout the afternoon, the students opened up and let their guard down. By the end, when I was signing certificates for their course completion, we were all friends. The Haddad twins, Kevin and Alan, drove me back to the hotel, pointing out places of reference. We chatted about their last few years bartending and their hopes for the future. Their genius with flavors and hospitality runs in their family.

That evening, we headed for a fantastic dinner filled with the most delicious food and drinks and a lot of flavored hookahs. At Central Station, we linked up with Jad Ballout, a great bartender, who shared his plans for a bar that was in the early stages of construction, Electric Bing Sutt. Jad had access to some cool old-meets-new equipment and products in Central Station's basement, including his rotovap and his portfolio of SCOBYs across the back wall producing his lineup of Booch for the bar.

The following day, Jad and his partner, Issey Lin, took me to their neighborhood café for lunch, followed by an afternoon of visiting spice shops and learning more about the local flavors. I was particularly mesmerized by the guy standing out on the street with a cardboard box filled with fresh peanuts in the shell, being roasted à la minute with a shovel and roaster that looked like a cement mixer. The pistachios and green almonds, though, oh my goodness. Those flavors live on in my dreams. Another key Lebanese flavor, Damascus rose, is among the most expensive essential oils in the world. We walked over to Jad and Issey's under-construction bar and had the "hard hat tour."

The Lebanese people are so kind and resilient, and the universe would put them to the test in the summer of 2020, when there was a massive fire and bomb explosion on the docks in downtown Beirut, devasting the city. Electric Sing Butt was one of many businesses affected by the tragedy. The international industry leapt to help, and I'm happy to report that Jad and Issey's new bar, Dead End Paradise, is now open.

I will always look back fondly on my trip to Beirut, not just because of the delicious food I ate, but also because the people and the landscape made it a truly once-in-a-lifetime experience.

Method

To a shaker, add the gin, eau de vie, crème de cacao, lemon juice, syrup, bitters, peanut butter, and egg white. Dry shake (without ice) for 5 seconds to emulsify the ingredients. Open the shaker and add cubed ice. Using some force, shake hard for 10 seconds. Using a small fine-mesh bar sieve to catch the loose ice chips, double strain into a chilled cocktail glass or coupe. Garnish with grated peanut.

Serves 1

Area of inspiration: Beirut, Lebanon
Inspired by: the Twentieth Century

———

1 ounce (30 mL) gin

½ ounce (15 mL) fraise eau de vie (or framboise)

½ ounce (15 mL) white crème de cacao

¾ ounce (22.5 mL) fresh lemon juice

1 ounce (30 mL) Simple Syrup (page 47)

2 dashes chocolate bitters
(like Bittered Sling Malagasy Chocolate)

1 bar spoon (3 g) powdered peanut butter

1 egg white (see note)

Garnish: Grated peanut

Note: If you are concerned about the food safety
of raw eggs, use 1 ounce (30 mL) pasteurized
liquid egg whites in place of the egg white.

Gin & Symphonic

It might seem a little crazy to create a cocktail inspired by Metallica, but creativity and imagination develop in unexpected areas. I have this vivid memory of my little brother, Jake, in high school, dressed in his Nirvana T-shirt, with bleach-blond hair, blasting "Enter Sandman" in his room. He'd be up all night, switching between singles on the 1991 *Metallica* album and yapping to his pals about movies on his Batmobile phone. Fast-forward to 1999 and the legendary San Francisco–based heavy metal band had partnered up with the award-winning San Francisco Symphony Orchestra for a collaborative rerelease of their *S&M* album. Progressive new renditions of classic Metallica tunes were brought to life with the intensity of a full orchestra—brass, percussion, woodwinds—proving once and for all that you can love classical and heavy metal music, together!. It's an incredible collaboration that still tickles the eardrums. I often associate music, art, color, and sound with cocktails and flavor, and the Gin & Symphonic cocktail was born from this idea. I created this drink for the Four Seasons Hotel San Francisco; the "Fog City Tales" menu was a compilation of stories celebrating the city's vibrant history and culture, a convergence of different ideas and attitudes. As in music, with the right balance, we can achieve perfect harmony when all the ingredients come together.

Method

To a shaker filled with cubed ice, add the gin, sherry, cordial, bitters, brine, and egg white. Using some force, shake hard for 5 seconds. Using a small fine-mesh bar sieve to catch the loose ice chips, double strain into a chilled cocktail glass or coupe. Garnish with the citrus coins, arranged in four points, like a square.

Serves 1

Area of inspiration: San Francisco, California
Inspired by: the Hotel Georgia

———

2 ounces (60 mL) gin

½ ounce (15 mL) fino sherry

1½ ounces (45 mL) California Citrus Cordial (page 92)

2 dashes lemon bitters
(like Bittered Sling Lem-Marrakech)

1 dash preserved lemon brine

1 egg white (see note)

Garnish: 4 small citrus coins (recipe follows)

Citrus Coins

To make the citrus coins, cut a strip of peel from each of a lemon, orange, grapefruit, and lime. Place the peel on a cutting board and push down with a ¾-inch (2 cm) circle cutter or small cookie cutter. Punch out one circle per fruit and set aside until ready to use.

Note: If you are concerned about the food safety of raw eggs, use 1 ounce (30 mL) pasteurized liquid egg whites in place of the egg white.

Gin-Gin Donkey Kong

Throughout the years, I've been following the Australian bar scene, and it's changed my perception of what's possible if you embrace where you are, creating menus based on ingredients you have access to, especially classic drinks with local twists, rather than holding out to make "a proper drink" because you're missing brand X. Bartenders in British Columbia think the same way: if you don't have it, make it—but don't just make it, fill the gap and make it the best in the show. When I was last in Australia, my friend Rairn Gill took me to meet many bartenders who are changing the game in Melbourne. Each bar boasted different dishes, drinks, modifiers, and flavors. It was one of those great moments when I could stop and appreciate the genius of the bartending profession within which I gratefully share space. No bar duplicated the tastes and experiences of another. I remember calling my friend, Anya Haarhoff, back in Amsterdam and telling her about this amazing treasure trove of talent. She said, "I knew when you left for Australia you'd want to stay there—it's extraordinary." The Gin-Gin Donkey Kong is a bit of a riff on the gin-gin mule by Audrey Saunders, one of the most famous New York bartenders, but was inspired by some of the loveliest flavor combinations I experienced in Melbourne. A huge thank you to the bartenders who showed me such love and kindness on that trip—it's safe to say I'm excited to come back one day.

Method

To a shaker filled with cubed ice, add the gin, vermouth, syrup, lemon juice, and bitters. Using some force, shake hard for 5 seconds. Using a small fine-mesh bar sieve to catch the loose ice chips, double strain into a Collins glass filled with cubed ice. Top with the tea and stir just to combine. For the garnish, thread the banana slice and mint onto a cocktail pick and place it across the top of the glass.

Serves 1

Area of inspiration: Melbourne, Australia
Inspired by: the Gin-Gin Mule

———

¾ ounce (22.5 mL) gin

¾ ounce (22.5 mL) Singularity Dark Vermouth (page 239) or Averna amaro

1 ounce (30 mL) Caramelized Banana Syrup (page 92)

¼ ounce (7.5 mL) fresh lemon juice

1 dash coffee bitters
(like Bittered Sling Arabica Coffee)

3 ounces (90 mL) chilled black tea, carbonated (see note)

Garnish: Banana slice, fresh mint sprig

Note: Use a carbonated drink maker like the Drinkmate to carbonate the tea.

Historically Famous

The Martinez was created by Jerry Thomas, the first professional bartender written into the books. He lived in San Francisco in the 1800s. A gin-based drink, the Martinez is a great recipe to recreate and reimagine from different influences, and I refer to it a lot in this book. I was inspired by Thomas and the hotel bar the Occidental (where he lived for a short while) to create a drink called the Occidentally Famous for the Four Seasons in San Francisco. The Historically Famous cocktail reimagines the Martinez (and the Occidentally Famous) from my current point of view as a resident of the Netherlands. It showcases the fruit and grain ingredients that originated in this country, specifically in the form of Genever. I have my friend Tess Posthumus to thank for welcoming me into the world of Genever here in the Netherlands. This recipe shows bartenders and cocktail lovers worldwide that we can create and reinvent cocktails based on our imagination and access. The original recipe acts as a guideline, and the classic's inventor provides inspiration for years to come. Thanks, Jerry Thomas, and to historian David Wondrich for bringing Thomas' story to the mainstream. I've reimagined this drink hundreds of times, and I'm not alone. It's a great design to work within.

Method

For the garnish, slice an orange wedge, and place skin side down on a baking sheet. Using a kitchen torch, lightly caramelize the orange's flesh on either side of the wedge. Use metal tongs to move the orange around. Once cooled, thread lengthwise on a pick, and set aside. Fill a mixing glass with cubed ice. Add the Genever, vermouth, eau de vie, liqueur, bitters, and saline solution. Stir with a bar spoon for 15 to 20 rotations. Using a julep strainer, strain into a Nick and Nora glass or coupette. Drape the torched orange skewer across the top of the glass rim.

Serves 1

Area of inspiration: Schiedam, Netherlands
Inspired by: the Martinez

———

2 ounces (60 mL) Genever or gin

¾ ounce (22.5 mL) Infrared Red Vermouth (page 238) or red vermouth

¼ ounce (7.5 mL) pear eau de vie (like Poire Williams)

¼ ounce (7.5 mL) apricot liqueur

2 dashes orange bitters (like Bittered Sling Orange & Juniper)

2 dashes Saline Solution (page 95)

Garnish: Thick orange wedge with peel intact

Kale & Nori

In 2011, Jonathan and I had a dream of opening our own business, but the money aspect was challenging. We didn't have access to funds, credit, or investors. Our parents gave us a small amount to help, but we relied heavily on working two or three jobs each while putting our dream together. Kale & Nori, our catering company and boutique events service, was born on July 24, 2011. Days later, our first gig brought us to Vancouver Island, to Courtney in the Comox Valley, to participate with other ocean lovers in the food and beverage industry at the BC Shellfish Festival. Along the way, Jonathan gave me a crash course in local flora and fauna, with an ocean view, as he'd started his cooking career at the Relais & Châteaux Aerie Resort on the island. We passed through mountains of white and gray chalk along the seashores, and the view sharpened into oyster shells— millions of them. The dunes moved up and down along the road, and we noticed something else: green bushes coming out of the tide. We pulled over, Jonathan grabbed a bowl and his kitchen scissors from his knife roll, and we walked over the dunes. It was sea asparagus, or samphire. We walked out into the low tide and started snipping. This moment was one of the first times I truly understood Jonathan's passion for all things aquaculture, and since then, he's helped this city kid become more connected to the ocean. When we eventually made it to the festival and met food writer Nathan Fong (our friend, who recently passed) for the first time, we were introduced to a whole world of food writers who would help us with our new company. On that trip, the drinks I made were inspired by the land (Kale), and the dishes Jonathan cooked with sea cucumbers and sea asparagus, were inspired by the sea (Nori). We set our company's name in stone that day, and since then, our respect for both land and sea has remained robust.

Serves 1

Area of inspiration: Vancouver Island, British Columbia
Inspired by: the Rose Cocktail

———

1 ounce (30 mL) gin

1 ounce (30 mL) Green Cameo Vermouth (page 238) or white vermouth

1 ounce (30 mL) green tea kombucha

½ ounce (15 mL) Ginger Shrub (page 93)

2 dashes grapefruit bitters
(like Bittered Sling Grapefruit & Hops)

Garnish: Pickled ginger, fresh basil leaf

Method

To a shaker filled with cubed ice, add the gin, vermouth, kombucha, shrub, and bitters. Using some force, shake hard for 5 seconds. Using a small fine-mesh bar sieve to catch the loose ice chips, double strain into a cocktail glass or coupe. For the garnish, thread pickled ginger onto a cocktail pick and serve on the side, and clip the basil leaf to the glass. It's lovely to enjoy this drink with a taste of the pickled ginger and the sip of the cocktail back and forth.

The Kasbah

Cars whizzed up and down the narrow cobblestone lanes around the medina entrances, just missing us at every turn. We twitched as scooters zipped in front of us at rapid speeds, each carrying three people and, sometimes, their groceries. It was an electric, organized chaos. Fashion designer Yves Saint Laurent once said about Morocco, "Marrakech taught me color. Before Marrakech, everything was black." He couldn't have been more right. The brightly colored buildings—cobalt blue, pink, yellow, purple—against the periwinkle-blue sky of Morocco are etched in my memory. As we ducked into shops for temporary solace from the blazing sun, our friends Luca and Kristine, Jonathan, and I were greeted with a magical sense of hospitality. Hot gold-rimmed glasses filled with fresh mint tea and a touch of sugar inspired me as spices wafted through the kasbah. Minutes turned to hours of shopping for handmade jewelry, rugs, and essential oils. In the mid-afternoon, the sun reflected from tile to tile as our host led us through the walls of an ancient medina. The call to prayer echoed in the background, and to my right, a family managing a roadside stand prepared freshly squeezed orange juice in recycled water bottles, providing a sweet blood-sugar boost for tourists and workers in the blistering sunshine and intense dry heat. The Kasbah cocktail tastes like the smells and flavors of that day in the markets and cafés of Tangier.

Serves 1

Area of inspiration: Tangier, Morocco
Inspired by: the Clover Club

————

2 ounces (60 mL) gin

¾ ounce (22.5 mL) Starlight White Vermouth (page 239) or white vermouth

1½ ounces (45 mL) Rose & Raspberry Cordial (page 94)

3 dashes lemon bitters
(like Bittered Sling Lem-Marrakech)

1 egg white (see note)

Garnish: 3 cucumber ribbons

Method

To a shaker filled with cubed ice, add the gin, vermouth, cordial, bitters, and egg white. Using some force, shake hard for 5 seconds. Using a small fine-mesh bar sieve to catch the loose ice chips, double strain into a cocktail glass or coupe. For the garnish, prepare 3 cucumber ribbons by moving a Y-shaped vegetable peeler toward you down the length of the cucumber until you get 3 nice wide strips (the first few will be too thin). Coil each ribbon into a spiral and thread it onto a cocktail pick, moving the previous one along as you add the next. Place the pick across the top of the glass.

Note: If you are concerned about the food safety of raw eggs, use 1 ounce (30 mL) pasteurized liquid egg whites in place of the egg white.

Late-Night Ramos

The Ramos gin fizz is a ritual for bartenders visiting New Orleans. The Ramos (as it is affectionately known) is the perfect breakfast, lunch, and mid-afternoon cocktail—but who says you can't have one before bed? Choose your timing carefully when ordering a Ramos; you must assess the number of bartenders versus the number of guests and make a judgment call, as you need to consider the five-minute preparation time. The best place to enjoy a properly made Ramos is at the Sazerac Bar at the Roosevelt Hotel, a legendary hotel bar and one of my favorite places in New Orleans. On a recent adventure in the city, my friend Rebecca Sturt and I headed to the Sazerac for a late-night Ramos—a slow time of day to order the drink without interruption. We have shared this ritual many times, and it's especially perfect over ghost stories in a haunted hotel like the Roosevelt. While the classic recipe is an amazing cocktail to savor, it does present a fun opportunity for creative adaptation. With a classic Ramos, I enjoy just one decadent glass, but this variation means I can have two (or maybe three). My Late-Night Ramos uses coconut cream instead of dairy, and adds the perfumed character of lemongrass and lime leaf. If you prefer, you can always choose to make it with heavy or whipping cream in place of the coconut cream.

Method

To a blender, add the ice, gin, syrup, egg white, coconut cream, xanthan gum, rose water, and lemon and lime juice. Blend on medium for 5 seconds, then high for 10 seconds. Pour into a chilled Collins glass. Top with club soda to create the soufflé. Serve with a reusable or compostable straw.

Serves 1

Area of inspiration: New Orleans, Louisiana
Inspired by: the Ramos Gin Fizz

———

3 ice cubes

1½ ounces (45 mL) gin

1 ounce (30 mL) Lemongrass & Lime Leaf Syrup (page 93)

1 egg white (see note)

1½ ounces (45 mL) coconut cream

⅛ tsp (¼ gram) xanthan gum

1 drop rose water

½ ounce (15 mL) fresh lemon juice

½ ounce (15 mL) fresh lime juice

Chilled club soda

Note: If you are concerned about the food safety of raw eggs, use 1 ounce (30 mL) pasteurized liquid egg whites in place of the egg white.

NEW ORLEANS

New Orleans is a cocktail mecca for bartenders, with drinks-industry stories and historical touches around every turn. Having been to New Orleans a dozen times over the last decade in many a gaggle of bartenders, I now know which bars have the best drinks and which landmarks in the French Quarter highlight essential dates in the cocktail birthday calendar. For example, in the 1830s, Antoine Amédée Peychaud created the Sazerac cocktail at the Sazerac Coffee House on Royal Street. In the 1850s, Joseph Santini created the brandy crusta at the Jewel of the South; in the 1870s, it was the absinthe frappé at the Old Absinthe House; and, of course, in the 1880s, the mighty Ramos gin fizz came along at the Imperial Cabinet Saloon. New Orleans is also the long-standing home of the Tales of the Cocktail Festival, the largest and longest-running cocktail conference in the world, attracting folks from all areas of the drinks industry once a year to attend seminars, network with like-minded people, and enjoy all that the city of jazz and hospitality has to offer.

The city is known for its history, and sure, the cocktails play a role, along with incredible Creole food blending French, Caribbean, Spanish, Italian, German, African, Portuguese, and Native American influences. But New Orleans is also the birthplace of jazz and is considered one of the best places to experience the trifecta of food, drink, and music. And we can't stop there—a supernatural world exists there that might not unfold in the plainness of day, but when the sun goes down, the streets and buildings start to talk. The most interesting and most relaxed moments in New Orleans happen after dark. With the stillness of the night and a great tour guide, you can experience the streets' stories.

Each neighborhood, each hotel, and each person you connect with in New Orleans has a story—part of the rich culture that has developed over more than three centuries. It has been the backdrop for many movies, books, civil rights movements, and more. The city speaks, and if you stop and listen, she might just talk to you.

Sea Basin Sbagliato

Nestled along the eastern Mediterranean Sea coast of Israel is Tel Aviv, a vibrant 24/7 culture of . . . everything! In the morning, I woke to piercing sunshine and took a walk along the boardwalk in the sea air. With a coffee and rugelach, my friend and fellow bartender Oron Lerner and I walked to the center of the city, through a huge market with walls seemingly made of halvah (the towers were that tall). At the top of the high street, we changed directions and headed toward a different district. There we met Adaya Lange, another great friend. She took us for a sidewalk lunch at her favorite vegetarian Iraqi sandwich stand: incredible flavors from nuts, seeds, grilled vegetables, and pickles, and the *best* bread. Later in the afternoon, I shared an apéritif on the north side of the city with my friend Ariel Leizgold, and we split some dishes at Fantastic in the Ballroom. As the night carried on, the city continued to wake up well into the early hours. I made a final stop at Jasper Johns to see some of the hardworking bartenders for a nip before bed, just as the bakeries were reopening. Each day in Tel Aviv is full of surprises, but the company we keep is the real treasure, and occasions with great friends are made even more extraordinary when there's a great drink to clink. The Sea Basin Sbagliato is a long, refreshing, and delightful cocktail inspired by some of the great flavors of Israel, with a lighter style and pink, bitter liqueur—lighter than the Campari style we're normally used to.

Method

Fill a mixing glass with cubed ice. Add the gin, vermouth, and bitter. Stir with a bar spoon for 15 to 20 rotations. Using a julep strainer, strain into a rocks glass filled with cubed ice. Top with sparkling wine and stir just to combine. Garnish with the cucumber slice.

Serves 1

Area of inspiration: Tel Aviv, Israel
Inspired by: the Negroni Sbagliato

——

¾ ounce (22.5 mL) gin

1¼ ounces (35 mL) Mellow Yellow Vermouth (page 238) or Cocchi Americano vermouth

1¼ ounces (35 mL) Sea Basin Bitter (page 9)

2 ounces (60 mL) chilled sparkling wine (full proof or nonalcoholic)

Garnish: 1 long cucumber slice (cut on an angle)

Smallage, Biggish

The Vesper is a cool cocktail—something fun that isn't as sweet as a Martinez and isn't as dry as a martini. It's the perfect in-between cocktail, with big potential. I often use the Vesper as a recipe template for a stirred drink since it's delicate on the nose and palate but offers the chance to hide ingredients in the nuances. The spin in this drink is all about celery, once called smallage when it stood tall as wild celery, long before it was domesticated into the sweet, manageable vegetable it is today. That's not to suggest that smallage or wild celery is my preference, but more that the flavor of celery in any form is a revelation in cooking and drinks; you just have to be bold enough to use it. The components here are flexible and give you lots of opportunities to twist and turn the recipe as you wish. Don't be afraid of celery; it's truly remarkable, and yes, I'm rather obsessed.

Method

Fill a mixing glass with cubed ice. Add the gin, aquavit, vermouth, brine, and both bitters. Stir with a bar spoon for 15 to 20 rotations. Using a julep strainer, strain into a Nick and Nora glass or coupette. For the garnish, use a peeler to remove a ribbon from a celery stalk (longer is better). Curl the ribbon and drop it into the glass. Use the peeler to remove a nice piece of peel from a washed lemon. Twist the peel to express the oil over the cocktail, then discard.

Serves 1

Area of inspiration: Western Canada
Inspired by: the Vesper Martini

———

1½ ounces (45 mL) gin

½ ounce (15 mL) aquavit

¾ ounce (22.5 mL) Green Cameo Vermouth (page 238) or Lillet aromatized wine

1 dash preserved lemon brine

1 dash celery bitters
(like Bittered Sling Cascade Celery)

1 dash orange bitters
(like Bittered Sling Orange & Juniper)

Garnish: Celery ribbon, lemon oil

Mise en Place Recipes

California Citrus Cordial

Makes 10 ounces (300 mL)

250 grams superfine or granulated sugar

8 grams grapefruit peel

7 grams orange peel

6 grams Meyer (or regular) lemon peel

5 grams lime peel

2½ ounces (75 mL) fresh grapefruit juice

2½ ounces (75 mL) fresh orange juice

2½ ounces (75 mL) fresh Meyer (or regular) lemon juice

2½ ounces (75 mL) fresh lime juice

2.5 grams citric acid

Add the sugar and peels to an airtight container and press with a muddler to release the oils. Cover and let stand for 24 hours. Transfer to a blender and add the citrus juices and citric acid. Blend on medium speed until the sugar is dissolved. Strain the liquid through a mesh sieve, then through cheesecloth to microfilter. Store in a sanitized bottle, labeled with the date, in the fridge for up to 10 days.

Caramelized Banana Syrup

Makes 10 ounces (300 mL)

150 grams Demerara sugar

5 ounces (150 mL) filtered water

150 grams banana (with peel), washed, dried, and sliced

Using an immersion circulator, bring a pot of water to 195°F (90°C) (or use a stem thermometer to hold the temperature on medium-high heat). In a bowl, whisk together the sugar and water until the sugar is dissolved. Add the banana slices to a heatproof food-safe bag and top with the sugar water. Remove the air from the bag, seal, and clip it to the side of the pot, ensuring that the mixture is underwater. Cook for 1½ hours. Transfer the bag to an ice bath and let cool. Strain the liquid into a sanitized bottle, label with the date, and store in the fridge for up to 10 days.

Ginger Shrub

Makes 16 ounces (500 mL)

One 3-inch (7.5 cm) piece fresh ginger

150 grams superfine or granulated sugar

5 ounces (150 mL) filtered water

5 ounces (150 mL) cane vinegar

Set up a juicer. Chop the ginger into small pieces. Run the ginger through the juicer, then strain the juice. You should have about 3½ ounces (100 mL) juice. Add the juice to a blender, along with the sugar, water, and vinegar. Blend on medium until the sugar is dissolved. Strain the liquid through a mesh sieve into a sanitized bottle, label with the date, and store in the fridge for up to 10 days.

Lemongrass & Lime Leaf Syrup

Makes 10 ounces (300 mL)

200 grams superfine or granulated sugar

7 ounces (200 mL) filtered water

2 grams fresh makrut lime leaves (about 10)

15 grams fresh lemongrass, chopped

Using an immersion circulator, bring a pot of water to 195°F (90°C) (or use a stem thermometer to hold the temperature on medium-high heat). In a bowl, whisk together the sugar and water until the sugar is dissolved. Add the lime leaves and lemongrass to a heatproof food-safe bag and top with the sugar water. Remove the air from the bag, seal, and clip it to the side of the pot, ensuring that the mixture is underwater. Cook for 1½ hours. Transfer the bag to an ice bath and let cool. Strain the liquid into a sanitized bottle, label with the date, and store in the fridge for up to 10 days.

Pumpkin Spice Ice Cream

Makes 16 ounces (500 mL)

1 cup (200 g) pumpkin puree

¾ cup (100 g) raw sugar

1 teaspoon (2 g) kosher salt

6 pieces cloves

¼ teaspoon (1 g) freshly grated nutmeg

2 cups (500 mL) 35% heavy cream

1 cup (250 mL) whole milk

1 vanilla bean, cut and scraped

8 egg yolks

¼ cup (50 g) white sugar

1 tablespoon (15 mL) aromatic bitters (like Bittered Sling Plum & Rootbeer Bitters)

1 tablespoon (15 mL) bourbon

Place the inner container of the ice cream maker in the freezer and let freeze overnight. The next day, in a medium saucepan on low heat, add the pumpkin puree, raw sugar, salt, cloves, and nutmeg, stirring constantly, for 10 to 15 minutes. Add the cream, milk, and vanilla bean (inner seeds only) to the pumpkin mix, increase the heat to medium, and stir often to ensure nothing sticks or burns. In a separate bowl, combine the egg yolks, white sugar, bitters, and bourbon. Once the pumpkin and dairy mix is simmering, slowly add 1 cup at a time of the hot mixture to the egg mixture in a slow and steady stream, whisking constantly to temper the eggs. Repeat until everything is combined. Whisk until cool, about 10 minutes, then strain through a fine-mesh sieve. Transfer the mixture to a container and refrigerate, covered, until chilled. Follow the ice cream maker's setting to continue.

Rose & Raspberry Cordial

Makes 10 ounces (300 mL)

200 grams superfine or granulated sugar

11 grams citric acid

7 ounces (200 mL) filtered water

100 grams fresh raspberries

3 grams dried edible roses

Using an immersion circulator, bring a pot of water to 195°F (90°C) (or use a stem thermometer to hold the temperature on medium-high heat). In a bowl, whisk together the sugar, citric acid, and water until the sugar is dissolved. Add the raspberries and roses to a heatproof food-safe bag and top with the sugar water. Remove the air from the bag, seal, and clip it to the side of the pot, ensuring that the mixture is underwater. Cook for 3 hours. Transfer the bag to an ice bath and let cool. Strain the liquid into a sanitized bottle, label with the date, and store in the fridge for up to 10 days.

Saline Solution

Makes 4 ounces (125 mL)

12.5 grams sea salt

4 ounces (125 mL) cold filtered water

In a small bowl, combine the salt and water, stirring until dissolved. Pour into a bottle with a pipette dropper, and label and date. Store in the fridge for up to 6 months.

———

Sea Basin Bitter

Makes 16 ounces (500 mL), 24% ABV

7¼ ounces (215 mL) orange-flavored vodka

2½ ounces (75 mL) Simple Syrup (page 47)

2¼ ounces (70 mL) Tawny Orange NA Vermouth (page 237)

2¼ ounces (70 mL) Calypso Coral NA Vermouth (page 236)

1¾ ounces (50 mL) Rose & Raspberry Cordial (page 94)

2 dashes grapefruit bitters (like Bittered Sling Grapefruit & Hops)

Add all ingredients to a small jar, close the lid, and shake. Infuse for 24 hours. Strain the liquid into a sanitized bottle and label with the date and ABV. Store indefinitely with your other room-temperature alcohols.

Tula Gingerbread Syrup

Makes 10 ounces (300 mL)

150 grams brown sugar

150 grams raw honey

15 grams gum arabic powder

Pinch kosher salt

8 ounces (250 mL) filtered water

2 ounces (50 mL) fresh ginger juice (from a 2-inch/5 cm piece ginger)

8 whole cloves, smashed

2 green cardamom pods, smashed

1 cinnamon stick, smashed

1 gram allspice berries, smashed

Using an immersion circulator, bring a pot of water to 195°F (90°C) (or use a stem thermometer to hold the temperature on medium-high heat). In a bowl, whisk together the sugar, honey, gum arabic, salt, water, and ginger juice until the sugars are dissolved. Add the cloves, cardamom, cinnamon, and allspice to a heatproof food-safe bag and top with the sugar water. Remove the air from the bag, seal, and clip it to the side of the pot, ensuring that the mixture is underwater. Cook for 1½ hours. Transfer the bag to an ice bath and let cool. Strain the liquid into a sanitized bottle, label with the date, and store in the fridge for up to 10 days.

Liqueur & Amaro

Camp Pal-o-Mine

In 2017, I visited San Juan, Puerto Rico, just four months after hurricanes Irma and Maria devasted the Caribbean. I was in shock. I was there to work with local bartenders and businessowners on a program that would help get their stories out to a broader audience in hopes that we could continue to support each other through hard times in our industry. With some supportive spirit brands behind us, we were able to share a three-part series on social media and YouTube that brought the drinks community together. It was called *The Pioneers*. Bartenders Carlos Irizarry (La Factoría) and Michael Norat (Santaella) and Chef María Grubb shared their stories. I was moved to tears listening to their accounts of courage and love. Later that week, I worked with bartenders from different regions, bars, and backgrounds; their drinks, stories, and presentations were so personal and emotional. The care the Puerto Rican bartending community showed for one another in some of the darkest hours impacted me profoundly, and their love for people and genuine hospitality continue to flow like an electric current in our industry. This drink represents one of the loveliest classics, the jungle bird (also the name of a wicked bar in San Juan).

Method

To a shaker filled with cubed ice, add the Campari, rum, tepache, lime juice, and syrup. Using some force, shake hard for 5 seconds. Shape the banana leaf to fit inside a double rocks or highball glass widthwise, with a bit sticking out the top. Add cubed ice to the glass. Strain the cocktail into the glass.

Serves 1

Area of inspiration: San Juan, Puerto Rico
Inspired by: the Jungle Bird

———

1 ounce (30 mL) Campari

1 ounce (30 mL) dark rum

1 ounce (30 mL) Pineapple Tepache (page 113)

½ ounce (15 mL) fresh lime juice

½ ounce (15 mL) Hibiscus Syrup (page 112)

Garnish: Banana, pandan, or sesame leaf

Chartreuse Milkshake

I came up with the Chartreuse Milkshake in 2008 while working at a Vancouver restaurant called Chow. Chow was owned by a then unknown and now super-famous chef named Jean-Christophe (J-C) Poirier, who went on to become a close friend. For the cocktail, I removed dairy entirely and worked on the relationship between the orange and egg white to create a magical texture that simulated the light touch of dairy. The components create an accessible, familiar, and delicious way for green Chartreuse to shine. Chartreuse is an herbal liqueur made by Carthusian monks in the mountains near Grenoble, north of Lyon, France. The liqueur was meaningful to me for several reasons. I was friends with the export director, Philippe Rochez (aka Green Fox), and I was always looking for interesting ways to bring Chartreuse into the mainstream. The liqueur is also a rite of passage in a bartender's education. Learning about Chartreuse opened up a world of flavors and spirits beyond the sports bars. Knowing the history, background, and ritual associated with Chartreuse, and the creativity that was possible with it, moved me into a different category of bartender, allowing me to delve into a group of spirits that were so much more than liquid in the glass. Since that day, this delicious cocktail has appeared in bars throughout Vancouver, Victoria, Whistler, Toronto, Munich, and Melbourne, along with a few books, including *Schofield's Fine and Classic Cocktails* by two legendary bartenders and friends, Joe and Daniel Schofield. I hope it will become a modern Canadian classic and continue to be enjoyed for years to come.

Serves 1

Area of inspiration: South Granville, Vancouver, British Columbia
Inspired by: the Twentieth Century

———

½ ounce (15 mL) green Chartreuse

1½ ounces (45 mL) gin

½ ounce (15 mL) white crème de cacao

¾ ounce (22.5 mL) fresh lime juice

¾ ounce (22.5 mL) fresh orange juice

½ ounce (15 mL) Simple Syrup (page 47)

2 dashes chocolate bitters
(like Bittered Sling Malagasy Chocolate)

1 egg white (see note)

Garnish: Cacao nibs, crushed

Method

To a shaker, add the Chartreuse, gin, crème de cacao, lime juice, orange juice, syrup, bitters, and egg white. Dry shake (without ice) for 5 seconds to emulsify the ingredients. Open the shaker and add cubed ice. Using some force, shake hard for 5 seconds. Using a small fine-mesh bar sieve to catch the loose ice chips, double strain into a Collins glass filled with cubed ice. Garnish with cacao nibs and serve with a reusable or compostable straw.

Note: If you are concerned about the food safety of raw eggs, use 1 ounce (30 mL) pasteurized liquid egg whites in place of the egg white.

Sour Roses

A few cocktails in this book are from my competition days, and that's to be expected. After all, so much of my creative flow was inspired by a specific event, challenge, ingredient, or related trip. The Sour Roses cocktail was part of Against the Clock, in which I was tasked with creating ten drinks in ten minutes or less. This challenge was very personal. Fifty-four bartenders competed that day, and with 500 live audience members and three microphone packs with cameras in my face, when my soundtrack came on (an impressive playlist DJ Eric Carver made for me of funk and disco tracks), I knew exactly where I needed to be in the timing, based on the songs' bars—I rehearsed a lot. The concept was a global trip showcasing the flavors and recipe designs that inspired some of my favorite drink menus in Vancouver. The Sour Roses represented my travels to Hawaii with its combination of coconut, flowers, and citrus. This is one of my personal favorites.

Method
To a shaker, add the Campari, vodka, syrup, lime juice, bitters, and egg white. Dry shake (without ice) for 5 seconds to emulsify the ingredients. Open the shaker and add cubed ice. Using some force, shake hard for 5 seconds. Using a small fine-mesh bar sieve to catch the loose ice chips, double strain into a coupe glass. Garnish with the rose.

Serves 1

Area of inspiration: Oahu, Hawaii
Inspired by: the Vodka Sour

———

1 ounce (30 mL) Campari

1 ounce (30 mL) Coconut Vodka with Roses (page 112)

1 ounce (30 mL) Toasted Coconut Syrup (page 67)

¾ ounce (22.5 mL) fresh lime juice

2 dashes cherry bitters
(like Bittered Sling Suius Cherry)

1 egg white (see note)

Garnish: Dried edible rose

Note: If you are concerned about the food safety of raw eggs, use 1 ounce (30 mL) pasteurized liquid egg whites in place of the egg white.

Westphalia

In 2015, I visited Wolfenbüttel, on the outskirts of Hannover, Germany. The dark, liquid Jägermeister has been produced there since 1935, and its traditions have existed since the early 1800s, when vinegar was the product manufactured. While there, I spent time with Nils Boese—not just a bartender and spirited snake-charmer, but a legendary ambassador to Germany's most famous export. At his 400-square-foot "home bar" in Hildesheim, Nils's endless back and front bars of ingredients from all over the world left little room to move around. The area was mapped out in such a way that only Nils himself could see, navigate, and remember the pickup points for each of the thousands of bottles across tables, counters, and shelves. I watched him gently grab bottle after bottle, with a cigarette hanging from his mouth, pouring without spouts or jiggers into a long line of mixing glasses. Effortlessly, fifteen mix-and-match glasses were collected and pushed to the workspace, and out came the finished product. Another critical moment in Nils's lesson: "Why do bartenders automatically garnish everything with orange, when lemon oils offer so much more on the nose?" I made the comparison, and he was right. Since that trip, I often use Jägermeister as a liqueur modifier in a drink and think critically about my citrus zest and the right time to use one over the other.

Method

Fill a mixing glass with cubed ice. Add the Jägermeister, gin, vermouth, and bitters. Stir with a bar spoon for 15 to 20 rotations. Using a julep strainer, strain into a Nick and Nora glass or coupette. For the garnish, use a peeler to remove a nice piece of peel from a washed lemon. Using a paring knife, trim the edges on all sides. Twist the peel to express the oil over the cocktail, then drop it into the glass.

Serves 1

Area of inspiration: Westphalia, Germany
Inspired by: the Hanky Panky

———

½ ounce (15 mL) Jägermeister

1½ ounces (45 mL) gin

¾ ounce (22.5 mL) Infrared Red Vermouth (page 238) or red vermouth

2 dashes lemon bitters
(like Bittered Sling Lem-Marrakech)

Garnish: Lemon twist

Bitter Brain Freeze

In 2011, Jonathan and I received excellent news: our bitters were to be featured at the first-ever bitters market at Tales of the Cocktail on Tour in Vancouver, British Columbia. This would be the first pop-up that would inspire further years of cocktail bitters–focused markets at the main Tales festival each year in New Orleans. We had work to do; our little company had just received permits to commercialize, our flavors were ready, and we had a huge order that would be hand-bottled (which we did for years). We called our friends Sabrine Dhaliwal and Layla Frances and pleaded for their bottling help. Many nights at our commercial kitchen above Campagnolo restaurant were spent filtering, refiltering, bottling, labeling, heat-sealing, and packaging Bittered Sling bitters for the marketplace. Sabrine, Evelyn Chick, Grant Sceney, David Wolowidnyk, Jay Jones, Trevor Kallies, Chantelle Gabino, and Nishantha Nepulongoda were part of the original Bittered Sling crew, working the pop-up restaurant and event scene with us for years, and are some of the best bartenders on the planet in their own right—both in talent and hospitality. They're just all-around good eggs. Over the years, the folks who believed in us became more than bartenders using our product; they became family. Without hesitation, the #bitterbabes, as they became known, would make time in their schedules to peel pallets of citrus fruits by hand, label our first packages for the US market, or represent Bittered Sling and Canada at numerous pop-ups around the world. We have the most amazing chosen family we could hope for, and it's still going strong today. As Bittered Sling continues to expand, one decade on, #bitterbabe has become a lifestyle tag as well as the mark of a truly amazing person. Thank you to our local and international #bitterbabes for all your support over the years. We feel the best is yet to come. A nostalgic drink with nostalgic flavors is the only drink appropriate for this crew.

Serves 1

Area of inspiration: North America
Inspired by: the Ice Cream Float

———

½ ounce (15 mL) chilled Fernet-Branca

1 ounce (30 mL) chilled bourbon

½ ounce (15 mL) chilled Cardamom Curaçao (page 46)

2 ounces (60 mL) chilled Root Beer Cordial (page 112)

2 dashes aromatic bitters
(like Bittered Sling Plum & Rootbeer)

4 ounces (125 mL) chilled sparkling coconut water (like La Croix)

2 small scoops coconut ice cream

Garnish: Toasted coconut flakes

Method

Make sure all the ingredients are ice cold before making this cocktail. To a Collins glass or glass beer mug, add the fernet, bourbon, curaçao, cordial, and bitters. Add 2 cubes of ice and stir to combine. Add coconut water until the glass is three-quarters full. Stir to combine. Gently add the ice cream (don't splash) and top with more coconut water. Garnish with coconut and serve with a reusable or compostable straw.

Buttered Oolong Toddy

In 2009, I was working at a bar on Granville Street in Vancouver's entertainment district, and there were always strange things happening in the area; it was the nature of the neighborhood. Of all the shenanigans that would occur in the back alley, my favorite was meeting Pedro Villalon, the tea hunter, for the first time. Pedro is originally from Mexico, and in addition to being a chemical engineer, he's one of the most brilliant, kind, and well-traveled tour guides in the world of rare teas. One night, he opened the trunk of his little car, and there it was: tea, tea, and more tea. Pedro specializes in teas procured directly from the source, working with farmers in far-flung regions of the world, and I was holding their precious gems in my hands. Pedro's company at the time was Dao Tea (*dao* means "the way"). I still have some of those original packages over a decade later—exceptional ones like the 2-pound (1 kg) puck of pu-erh tea from Yunnan province, China, and a 1991 oolong tea, barrel-aged in red wine casks, that tastes like coconut Nanaimo bars. Pedro has supported me so much, and I've listed a lot of his rare teas during special drink rituals and other moments when our guests could appreciate the work of tea artisans. Over the last ten years, Pedro and I have worked on countless projects together. In 2012, he opened O5 Rare Tea Bar in Vancouver, and it continues to operate today, cherishing the communities that brought the teas to our cups. I had the chance to share a story and cocktail inspired by Pedro at a bartending competition in Chicago. Like any great storyteller, Pedro has the power to transport us to a county in South Korea through a cup of really good tea.

Serves 1 to 2

Area of inspiration: Hwagae Market, Gyeongsangnam, South Korea
Inspired by: the Hot Toddy

———

8 ounces (250 mL) water

4 grams high-quality oolong tea leaves
(like O5's Balhyocha Noeul)

2 ounces (60 mL) amaro (like Amaro Lucano)

2 dashes chocolate bitters
(like Bittered Sling Malagasy Chocolate)

15 grams raw honey

1 teaspoon (5 mL) unsalted butter

Method

First brew the tea, using Pedro's recommended procedure: Boil the water to 185°F (85°C), add the tea, and steep for exactly 2 minutes. (While you can steep this tea multiple times, we want to use the first steep for the cocktail.) Strain the tea and add 3 ounces (90 mL) to a small clay teapot. Meanwhile, in a small saucepan, bring the amaro, bitters, honey, and butter to a simmer. Once simmering, add to the teapot. Pour small portions into clay teacups.

Tinto Naranja

In August 2018, Jonathan and I went to Seville, Spain, with a few friends. We had no idea it was the hottest place in continental Europe and almost totally closed up for the summer. But while the city was deserted midday, the early mornings and late nights were perfect: a light breeze, a beautiful temperature, and endless discoveries, tapas, produce, and Iberico ham. The drink we consumed the most during that trip was a blend of fresh Spanish citrus fruit, bone-dry fino sherry (procured on a day trip to Bodegas Lustau in Jerez de la Frontera), bitters, and tonic. Even out in bars, we braved the horrified looks while ordering "*dos vasos de Jerez-Manzanilla y dos botellas de tónica*." The faces were priceless, but we were happy. The simple drink tinto de verano (summer red wine, a combination of red wine and lemon soda over ice) inspired this recipe, along with Seville's famous orange wines. It's no wonder that Seville oranges appear in many beverages and spirits: the citrus tastes like the juiciest candy, with perfect flavor and balance. Making your own orange amargo at home is super easy, and you can enjoy it over several months.

Method

To a wineglass filled with cubed ice, add the amargo, shrub, sherry, and bitters. Stir gently with a bar spoon to chill. Add more ice if required; it should be right to the top. Add the tonic water and stir just to combine. Garnish with the orange wheel.

Serves 1

Area of inspiration: Seville, Spain
Inspired by: the Sherry Highball

———

¾ ounce (22.5 mL) Orange Amargo (page 113)

¾ ounce (22.5 mL) Kumquat Shrub (page 113)

¾ ounce (22.5 mL) manzanilla (or fino) sherry

1 dash orange bitters
(like Bittered Sling Orange & Juniper)

Chilled tonic water

Garnish: Orange wheel

Mise en Place Recipes

Coconut Vodka with Roses

Makes 8 ounces (250 mL), 40% ABV

8 ounces (250 mL) coconut vodka

3 grams dried edible roses

Add the vodka and roses to a jar, close the lid, and shake. Infuse for 3 hours. Strain the liquid into a sanitized bottle, pressing out liquid from the flowers. Label the bottle with the date and ABV. Store indefinitely with your other room-temperature alcohols.

———

Root Beer Cordial

Makes 16 ounces (500 mL)

150 grams dark brown sugar

10 ounces (300 mL) water

3½ ounces (100 mL) maple syrup

1¾ ounces (50 mL) blackstrap molasses

1 cinnamon stick

1 whole nutmeg, crushed

14 grams citric acid

10 grams sarsaparilla bark

2 grams birch bark

1 drop pure bergamot essential oil (see note)

Using an immersion circulator, bring a pot of water to 195°F (90°C) (or use a stem thermometer to hold the temperature on medium-high heat). In a bowl, whisk together the sugar, water, maple syrup, and molasses until the sugars are dissolved. Add the cinnamon stick, nutmeg, citric acid, sarsaparilla, birch, and essential oil to a heatproof food-safe bag and top with the sugar water. Remove the air from the bag, seal, and clip it to the side of the pot, ensuring that the mixture is underwater. Cook for 1½ hours. Transfer the bag to an ice bath and let cool. Strain the liquid into a sanitized bottle, label with the date, and store in the fridge for up to 10 days.

Note: Use only natural, pure bergamot essential oil (no carrier oils) and use a pipette to add a single drop. The oil is highly concentrated, and 1 drop is more than enough to aromatize. Store essential oils in the fridge in sealed containers.

———

Hibiscus Syrup

Makes 10 ounces (300 mL)

200 grams superfine or granulated sugar

7 ounces (200 mL) filtered water

3 grams dried hibiscus flowers (also called Jamaica, roselle, or sorrel)

In a small saucepan, combine the sugar and water. Bring to a slow simmer over medium heat, then immediately remove from the heat. (You don't want it to boil; this is just to dissolve the sugar.) In a heatproof container, using a mallet or muddler, break up the hibiscus flowers. Pour the sugar water over the flowers, but do not stir; let them infuse their flavor without disrupting the pigment release. After 15 minutes, strain the liquid through a fine-mesh sieve into a sanitized bottle. Label with the date and store in the fridge for up to 7 days.

Kumquat Shrub

Makes 10 ounces (300 mL)

200 grams superfine or granulated sugar (or raw white honey)

100 grams kumquats, sliced

3½ ounces (100 mL) filtered water

3½ ounces (100 mL) cane vinegar

1 drop natural orange food coloring (optional)

Add the sugar and kumquats to an airtight container and press with a muddler. Let stand for 24 hours. The next day, add the water and vinegar, stirring until the sugar is dissolved. If desired, add food coloring and whisk to combine. Strain the liquid into a sanitized bottle, label with the date, and store in the fridge for up to 10 days.

———

Orange Amargo

Makes 10½ ounces (315 mL), 24% ABV

4½ ounces (140 mL) Tawny Orange NA Vermouth (page 237)

3½ ounces (100 mL) dark rum

1 ounce (30 mL) amontillado sherry

1½ ounces (45 mL) Jaffa Orange Crush Cordial (page 185)

5 dashes orange bitters (like Bittered Sling Orange & Juniper)

Add all ingredients to a small jar, close the lid, and shake. Infuse for 24 hours. Strain the liquid into a sanitized bottle and label with the date and ABV. Store indefinitely with your other room-temperature alcohols.

Pineapple Tepache

Makes 1½ quarts (1.5 L)

110 grams superfine or granulated sugar

1½ quarts (1.5 L) cold filtered water

1 pineapple

In a large bowl, whisk together the sugar and water until the sugar is dissolved. Peel and core the pineapple and reserve the flesh for another use. Cut the peels and core into 3-inch (7.5 cm) pieces and add to a 2-quart (2 L) jar, preferably with an air lock (see note). Top with the sugar water. Fold a paper coffee filter in half and place on top of the fruit, pressing to soak, to keep the fruit submerged and moist. Close the lid. After 5 days, strain the liquid and filter into smaller bottles with rubber flip tops using a medium-sized fine-mesh sieve. Label with the date and store in the fridge for up to 6 months, burping every few days. Reserve some of the SCOBY for a future Pineapple Tepache starter.

Note: If you don't have a jar with an air lock, just close the lid and remember to "burp" the jar each day to release the carbon dioxide, a by-product of fermentation.

Rum

Flora Fashion

I recently asked my friend Lorena Vásquez, the legendary master blender for a Guatemalan Rum, "What is the most amazing thing about Guatemala?" She replied, without hesitation, "Lauren, it's always springtime." For those who live in a four seasons climate, those first few days coming out of a dark and cold hibernation are some of the best. Springtime feels like the light at the end of the tunnel, each person's rebirth into "what this year will represent"—the cleaning out of the proverbial (or literal) closet, our much-needed sunshine absorption, and re-emergence into nature. But in Guatemala, Lorena explained, the colors, flowers, aromas, and ingredients are always in full swing. The country has nineteen diverse ecosystems and thirty national parks that protect and cover cultural and natural reserves from forests to jungles, beaches to mountains and volcanoes, with thousands of plant species, birds, and animals. When it comes to expressing springtime through dishes and drinks, not everything needs to be about flowers; rather, think about a plant's life cycle, from seed to stalk to flower. In this case, the stages are represented by cacao beans, sugarcane, and lavender flowers.

Method

Fill a mixing glass with cubed ice. Add the rum, syrup, and bitters. Stir with a bar spoon for 15 to 20 rotations. Using a julep strainer, strain over a large ice cube in a rocks glass. For the garnish, use a peeler to remove a nice piece of peel from a washed grapefruit. Using a paring knife, trim the edges on all sides. Twist the peel to express the oil over the cocktail, then drop it into the glass.

Serves 1

Area of inspiration: Quetzaltenango, Guatemala
Inspired by: the Old Fashioned

———

2 ounces (60 mL) Guatemalan rum

½ ounce (15 mL) Lavender Syrup (page 67)

2 dashes chocolate bitters
(like Bittered Sling Malagasy Chocolate)

Garnish: Grapefruit twist

Peak Me Up

In 2013, I wrote a beverage program for the Four Seasons Hotel Vancouver focused on raising awareness about the world's lakes, oceans, and water systems and educating guests through great cocktails that would bring the stories to life. I couldn't know at the time that my pitch to the powers that be would set up quite a few programs for me over the next seven years. In 2017, the team in Whistler, British Columbia, contacted me. They loved the Oceans Program in Vancouver and wondered what would be possible for the mountains. I was thrilled and pitched an idea called "Spirit of the Mountains"—volcanoes, craters, windows to the heavens, and our intrinsic connection to them. This global-feeling program brought the stories of different mountainous regions to Whistler for guests to learn and enjoy while relaxing at the hotel during their mountain getaway. One of my favorite drink stories involves Africa's tallest peak, Mount Kilimanjaro. The rich orange Tanzanian soil in the surrounding area gives us excellent coffee, bananas, and spices. A drink works best when at least one ingredient from a region is spotlighted—that is how we truly honor the area. We can "visit" these places by supporting and tasting products from local communities. Luckily, there are great companies out there, like Level Ground, that provide single-origin fair-trade products. Procuring regional coffee is the best place to start. My friend Nicola Riske and I have often talked about doing the hike to Kilimanjaro's summit and seeing this place for ourselves. We hope to have the opportunity one day, but in the meantime we can travel through the glass.

Method

To a shaker filled with cubed ice, add the rum, vermouth, liqueur, coffee, nectar, and bitters. Using some force, shake hard for 10 seconds. Using a small fine-mesh bar sieve to catch the loose ice chips, double strain into a clay cup. For the garnish, place the banana pyramid on a wooden hors d'oeuvre spoon and lay across the top of the cup.

Serves 1

Area of inspiration: Mt. Kilimanjaro, Tanzania
Inspired by: the Espresso Martini

———

1 ounce (30 mL) Spiced Rum (page 133)

1 ounce (30 mL) Singularity Dark Vermouth (page 239) or Averna amaro

½ ounce (15 mL) banana liqueur

2 ounces (60 mL) cold brewed coffee

½ ounce (15 mL) coconut flower nectar

3 dashes spicy aromatic bitters
(like Bittered Sling Moondog Latin)

Garnish: Caramelized banana pyramid (recipe follows)

Caramelized Banana Pyramid

Wash an unpeeled banana, then slice on an angle all the way through. Move the knife 1 inch (2.5 cm) away, then slice on the opposite angle to create a pyramid shape. Place raw, superfine, or granulated sugar on a shallow plate and spread it out flat. Gently press the banana flesh down on the sugar until the sugar sticks. Repeat on the other side. Place the banana on a heatproof plate. Using a kitchen torch on the lowest setting, caramelize each side until golden brown.

Varuna Coffee

During a magical trip to India, I met so many talented people, each with their own stories, family traditions, and regional influences that came through in the flavors and spices of their drinks as well as in the presentation. I have always loved visiting markets and local hot spots with bartenders, as it feels like they're taking me on a trip through their daily routines; ones that are very different to my own. On this trip, I saw the vastness of flavors available in India, and realized that each area, bartender and custom cocktail was completely different to the next. The cocktail I created to celebrate these incredible ah-ha moments is influenced by wonderful bartenders like like Minakshi Singh, Khushnaz Raghina, Devi Singh Bhati, Jeet Rana, Rohan Rege, and Gaurav Dhyan. It's called the Varuna Coffee, and appeared on the Four Seasons Hotel Vancouver menu. It might sound like a traditional Vietnamese-style coffee, but the cold brew, sweet milk, and rum create a beautiful milk punch–style cocktail more in line with the ingredients I came across in India. Cheers to you, bartenders of India; you've inspired me in more ways than I can ever share.

Method

To a shaker filled with cubed ice, add the rum, coffee, syrup, and bitters. Using some force, shake hard for 10 seconds. Using a small fine-mesh bar sieve to catch the loose ice chips, double strain into a highball glass filled with cubed ice and sprinkle with cardamom. Serve with assorted Indian sweets on the side, if desired.

Serves 1

Area of inspiration: New Delhi, India
Inspired by: the Milk Punch and the Vietnamese Coffee

———

1 ounce (30 mL) Spiced Rum (page 133)

6 ounces (175 mL) chilled Strong Cardamom Coffee (page 133)

½ ounce (15 mL) Milk Syrup (page 132)

2 dashes aromatic bitters
(like Bittered Sling Kensington)

Garnish and Side: Freshly grated cardamom, assorted Indian sweets (optional)

Volcan de Masaya

You really can't appreciate the power of a volcano until you've set foot on one. While I was in Nicaragua on a trip with other bartenders, we drove past what seemed like an endless field of black rocks, with hay and straw sprouting in every direction. After an eruption 1,000 years earlier, scattered ash and buried lands preserved in lava flowed out to the highway. I could see the volcano's peak in the distance. As we neared the base of the volcano, our guide hollered, "*Vamos a la cima*!" ("Let's drive to the top!"). The ascension was quick. I thought the van would topple over from the steep incline, but with a few words of encouragement (I think I can, I think I can), the van made it to the summit. Looking back, I realize now how dangerous this particular field trip was—sticking my face in the crater, knowing the volcano was active! My mother is, no doubt, reading this for the first time, and I'm expecting a phone call any second telling me how silly I was to put myself in harm's way like that. Amid severe winds, I signed my name on a giant wooden pole that towered over the crater. I'm sure I've got a "Beyoncé-inspired wind-machine" photo of this somewhere, but I'll bet her hair didn't smell like sulfur. I will always remember looking into the crater, seeing the Earth's crust breathing like it had a pulse. The Volcan de Masaya cocktail represents the flavors from this trip. The smoke billowing from the smoking box is connected to the ethereal moment of being close to the sheer power of Mother Nature, who might come to life when we least expect it. If you don't have access to the applewood chips, smoking box, and handheld smoker, you can still make and enjoy this cocktail.

Serves 1

Area of inspiration: Masaya, Nicaragua
Inspired by: the Bobby Burns

———

1½ ounces (45 mL) aged rum

½ ounce (15 mL) amontillado sherry

½ ounce (15 mL) cherry liqueur

½ ounce (15 mL) amaro (like Averna)

2 dashes cherry bitters
(like Bittered Sling Suius Cherry)

Garnish: Lemon twist, applewood chips (optional)

Method
Fill a mixing glass with cubed ice. Add the rum, sherry, liqueur, amaro, and bitters. Stir with a bar spoon for 15 to 20 rotations, until well chilled and diluted. Using a julep strainer, strain over a large ice cube in a rocks glass. For the garnish, use a peeler to remove a nice piece of peel from a washed lemon. Using a paring knife, trim the edges on all sides. Twist the peel between your fingers to express the oil over the cocktail, then drop it into the glass.

For an added bonus, fill a handheld smoker chamber with applewood chips and ensure it is connected securely to the smoking box (jar or cake dome) via the hose connector. Place the cocktail in the smoking box and close and latch the door. Turn on the handheld smoker and let the chamber fill with smoke for 20 seconds. Remove and enjoy.

São Paulo Swizzle

Did you ever fall in love with the idea of a place as a child, hoping someday to visit? Brazil was that place for me. Nothing felt farther away to this little girl living in Toronto with her brothers. I think my stepdad, Cliff, was the one who filled my head with the stories of his countless travels to Brazil. I was so obsessed with the idea that in the eighth grade, when I was fourteen years old, I wrote a novel for my English class called *The Feathered Nest*. A Brazilian-based narrative filled with adventure, it was a whimsical story from the imagination of a teenager who longed to discover and understand other places and meet new people. Years later, when I finally touched down in Brazil for the first time, it felt cathartic. I have been fortunate enough to travel to Brazil many times, and each experience gave me more insight into the culture, the importance Brazilians place on family, and, of course, the unique ingredients cultivated in the region. The São Paulo Swizzle is a blend of the flavors I encountered on my first visit: sugarcane, coffee, nuts, and citrus fruit.

Method

Add cubed ice to a Lewis bag and smash into chips with a mallet. Fill a large Collins glass (13- to 15-ounce/400 to 450 mL capacity) halfway with crushed ice and add the cachaça, soda, syrup, lime juice, and bitters. Stir with a swizzle stick or bar spoon to blend. Add more crushed ice to fill right to the top. Garnish with grated coffee, mint, and sugarcane. Serve with a long, wide reusable or compostable straw.

Serves 1

Area of inspiration: Centro Histórico de São Paulo, São Paulo, Brazil
Inspired by: the Queen's Park Swizzle

———

1½ ounces (45 mL) silver cachaça

1 ounce (30 mL) guarana soda (available in specialty stores) or club soda

¾ ounce (22.5 mL) Kola Nut & Cascara Syrup (page 132)

¾ ounce (22.5 mL) fresh lime juice

2 dashes coffee bitters
(like Bittered Sling Arabica Coffee)

Garnish: Grated coffee beans, fresh mint sprig, sugarcane stick

Juicy Fruit

The idea for this cocktail came to me after chatting with Ana Luiza Trajano, a Brazilian chef and culinary school instructor. We were working on a collaborative dinner in São Paulo, and I loved her passion for educating others on indigenous products from Brazil. I oohed and aahed as she scooped and smeared slow-cooked coconut milk and egg yolk custard onto a plate and topped it with meringue and crunchy bits. What struck me, though, wasn't just the way Chef Ana and her team handled the ingredients and spoke about the food, but how she created a family from her brigade—the covenant of the cook, where each position in the team is just as important as the executive chef. The group came together, held hands, and bowed their heads before guests were welcomed inside and the service began. It's beautiful to see these moments bloom in the open kitchen, with guests losing themselves in the creative energy. Chef Ana's children were sitting at the huge communal table next to guests, tasting every bite with intrigue and chatting with big, excited smiles. That's the best way for food and beverages to be enjoyed—with genuine conviviality. The Juicy Fruit highlights a classic Brazilian cocktail, evolved with some of the Brazilian ingredients showcased in Chef Ana's books, which she lovingly gifted to me on the last day of our work together. Obrigada, Chef!

Method

To a metal tin or glass Boston shaker, add the cachaça, lime and tangerine wedges, sugar, and passion fruit pulp. Press with a muddler. Add some ice and shake hard, then dump the contents into a highball glass, topping with more ice if necessary. Garnish with mint.

Serves 1

Area of inspiration: Liberdade, São Paulo, Brazil
Inspired by: the Caipirinha

——

2 ounces (60 mL) silver cachaça

½ lime (with peel), cut into 4 wedges

½ tangerine (with peel), cut into 4 wedges

20 grams raw cane sugar

15 grams sweet passion fruit pulp

Garnish: Fresh mint

Dancing Queen

My mom, Linda, is one of the greatest inspirations in my life. I come from a long line of headstrong women, chock-full of entrepreneurial spirit and emotional intelligence (almost to their detriment), with such a connected way of working with people, business, and passions. I didn't realize how hard it was for my mom when I was young, but as I grew older, I learned more about who she was as she let down her guard. Recently, she shared a story about her time as a professional model in Europe, and a specific program she worked on in the former Yugoslavia. The show featured futuristic and fantastic garments, silver jumpsuits, and blaring ABBA music. The crowd was pumped, and the photographer had slipped a little bottle of slivovitz—the Eastern European plum brandy—into the pocket of each outfit. As each model took a swig of liquid courage, they landed on the runway with attitude and explosive energy that even Federico Fellini, who sat in the audience, could feel from a mile away. "Dancing Queen" by ABBA always brings back a flood of memories for my mom, whether she's dancing in the living room, as we often do, or mixing a drink that reminds her of those days in 1976. This drink is a combination of my mom's favorite ingredients, in a delicate glass that symbolizes the feat of strength required for dancing in expensive outfits without spilling. And Linda loves a side serve—enjoy any white chocolate bon bon on the side.

Method

To a shaker filled with cubed ice, add the rum, crème de cacao, blueberry puree, syrup, lemon juice, and bitters. Using some force, shake hard for 10 seconds. Strain neat into a cocktail glass or coupe. Garnish with a lavender sprig threaded with 3 blueberries across the top of the glass.

Serves 1

Area of inspiration: Toronto, Ontario, via the former Yugoslavia (today, Croatia)
Inspired by: the Aviation

———

1 ounce (30 mL) white rum

½ ounce (15 mL) white crème de cacao

2 ounces (60 mL) blueberry puree

¾ ounce (22.5 mL) Lavender Syrup (page 67)

¾ ounce (22.5 mL) fresh lemon juice

2 dashes chocolate bitters
(like Bittered Sling Malagasy Chocolate)

**Garnish: Dried food-grade lavender sprig,
3 blueberries**

Miami Stucco Machine

Back in 2016 at an event in Miami, a few of us did a late night bar crawl, including stops at Sweet Liberty, Broken Shaker, and the lobby at One Hotel. Feeling quite hot, and wanting a dip in the pool, we headed to the Standard (one of my favorite hotels in the world) on Venetian Island. The Standard has a huge patio with sun loungers, two pools, three bars, and great little rooms (some with private outdoor hot tubs), and is right on the edge of the water. You'd swear time just stands still while you are there, but the mosquitoes soon shake you out of the dream—at dawn and dusk, you can avoid getting eaten alive by these night hawks only by hiding indoors (which you would never do) or submerging yourself in the lightly chlorinated water in the pool. In the wee hours of the morning, this was definitely the case. With the evening's cocktails still coursing through our veins and some blow-up pool toys, Simon, Grant, and I floated for hours under the full moon and starlight, having random conversations about fruit, politics, and water skiing. I gave this cocktail its name because each time we'd get up to change positions on the floaty toys, our knees, toes, and feet would graze the bottom of the pool, which for some reason was unfinished cement stucco! We didn't realize it until the next day, when our perfect South Beach bods and outfits were marred by Band-Aids covering scrapes and cuts! But it's all manageable if you have a frosé in hand, which the Standard is famous for. If I had to do it all again, I might have worn socks in the pool, but who does that? The scars are a reminder that good times might be accompanied by a bit of pain. This frosé is built for a crowd. I love large-format drinks, but you might want to bring along some bandages as a side serve, and don't forget the great tunes.

Serves 12

Area of inspiration: South Beach, Miami, Florida
Inspired by: Sangria

——

6 ounces (175 mL) white rum

9 ounces (275 mL) rosé wine

9 ounces (275 mL) Hibiscus Agua Fresca
(page 132)

6 ounces (175 mL) White Grape Cordial
(page 133)

9 dashes peach bitters
(like Bittered Sling Clingstone Peach)

Garnish: Sliced grapes, fresh mint

Method

In a large food-safe container, combine the rum, wine, agua fresca, cordial, and bitters, mixing well. Pour into sanitized bottles, label with the date, and store for up to 7 days.

For one serving, add 5 ounces (150 mL) of the mix to a blender, add 5 ice cubes, and blend on medium until smooth. Pour into a wineglass and top with grapes and mint. Serve with a reusable or compostable straw.

Mise en Place Recipes

Hibiscus Agua Fresca

Makes 1 quart (1 L)

5 grams dried hibiscus flowers (sometimes called Jamaica, roselle, or sorrel)

1 quart (1 L) cold filtered water

Place the flowers in a large food-safe container and pour water overtop. Stir, cover, and infuse in the fridge overnight. The next day, strain through a mesh sieve into a sanitized bottle, label with the date, and store in the fridge for up to 10 days.

———

Kola Nut & Cascara Syrup

Makes 16 ounces (500 mL)

300 grams Demerara sugar

10 ounces (300 mL) filtered water

5 grams cascara (dried coffee husks) or coffee beans

3 grams kola nut

In a small saucepan over low heat, combine the sugar and water, stirring until the sugar is dissolved. Add the cascara and kola nut. Bring to a boil, then turn off the heat, cover, and steep until cool. Strain the liquid through a mesh sieve, then through cheesecloth to microfilter. Store in a sanitized bottle, labeled with the date, in the fridge for up to 10 days.

Milk Syrup

Makes 16 ounces (500 mL)

½ vanilla bean

1 can (11¼ ounces/320 grams) condensed coconut milk or condensed milk

5½ ounces (165 mL) filtered water

Split the vanilla bean and scrape out the seeds, reserving the bean to make vanilla extract (see note). In a small saucepan over low heat, bring the coconut milk and water to a low simmer. Add the vanilla seeds and simmer for 3 to 5 minutes. Transfer to a heatproof container and let cool, then cover and infuse for 24 hours in the fridge. The next day, strain the liquid through a mesh sieve into a sanitized bottle, label with the date, and store in the fridge for up to 10 days.

Note: Reserve the scraped vanilla bean in an 8-ounce (250 mL) jar filled with dark rum. Cover and infuse indefinitely to make vanilla extract. Continue to add vanilla beans as you use them.

Spiced Rum

Makes 8 ounces (250 mL), 40% ABV

2 whole cloves

½ cinnamon stick

⅛ vanilla bean

1 gram allspice berries

1 gram whole black peppercorns

8 ounces (250 mL) dark rum

Add all ingredients to a small jar, close the lid, and shake. Infuse for 24 hours. Strain the liquid into a sanitized bottle and label with the date and ABV. Store indefinitely with your other room-temperature alcohols.

———

Strong Cardamom Coffee

Makes 26 ounces (800 mL)

4 green cardamom pods, smashed

30 grams coarsely ground coffee

26 ounces (800 mL) cold filtered water

Place the cardamom and coffee in a French press. Bring the water to a slow simmer (do not boil), then pour into the press. Stir and cover the top, without plunging. Infuse for 3 hours, then push down the plunger. Strain the coffee through a mesh sieve, then through cheesecloth to microfilter. Store in a sanitized bottle, labeled with the date, in the fridge for up to 10 days.

White Grape Cordial

Makes 10 ounces (300 mL)

200 grams superfine or granulated sugar

5 grams tartaric acid

5¾ ounces (170 mL) white verjuice

1 ounce (30 mL) champagne vinegar

In a bowl, whisk together the sugar, tartaric acid, verjuice, and champagne vinegar until the sugar is dissolved. Store in a sanitized bottle, labeled with the date, in the fridge for up to 10 days.

Vodka

Cosmonauts 1 & 2

In 2018, Charles Joly and I traveled to Moscow for a bartender training series, and we decided to visit Saint Petersburg together afterwards. Moscow was terrific. It was freezing (around −13°F/−25°C), but we had the right clothes and were happy to see the sights, like Red Square and Saint Basil's Cathedral, after our training finished. The next day, we headed north to Saint Pete's. It was even colder, and we were not prepared. On our only full day there, after trying to brave the elements at an outdoor flea market (we both have a passion for antiques), we found a local café and stepped in for a coffee and a vatrushka (a bun stuffed with baked cottage cheese and jam). It was so cold that someone wearing a parka at an outdoor flea market bought another parka to wear on top, all while Charles and I negotiated prices on vintage watches and bar gear. Tequila is almost always the narrator for my escapades with Charles, but for this story, vodka and traditional Russian fare were our guides. Our drink, one of the classic cocktail staples for any bartender, was the Cosmopolitan. This version is inspired by Russia's love of vodka and winter fruit, which always plays a role in their culture. The combo of cranberry juice and vodka with other winter modifiers makes it a truly unique cosmopolitan, a fitting tribute to our sub-zero Russian adventure.

Method

To a shaker filled with cubed ice, add the vodka, cranberry juice, syrup, and lemon juice. Using some force, shake hard for 5 seconds. Using a small fine-mesh bar sieve to catch the loose ice chips, double strain into a carbonated drink maker (like a Drinkmate). Add the filtered water and follow the manufacturer's instructions to carbonate. Gently release the pressure and pour into a Collins glass filled with cubed ice. For the garnish, use a peeler to remove a nice piece of peel from a washed orange. Using a paring knife, trim the edges on all sides. Twist the peel to express the oil over the cocktail, then drop it into the glass. Serve with gingerbread cookies on the side.

Serves 1

Area of inspiration: Moscow and Saint Petersburg, Russia
Inspired by: the Cosmopolitan

———

1½ ounces (45 mL) vodka

2 ounces (60 mL) natural sugar-free cranberry juice

1 ounce (30 mL) Tula Gingerbread Syrup (page 95)

½ ounce (15 mL) fresh lemon juice

1 ounce (30 mL) cold filtered water

Garnish and Side: Orange twist, Tula gingerbread cookies

Double-Double Caesar

For this ultra-Canadian drink, I wanted to bring together two of Canada's most beloved favorites: a Tim Hortons double-double and my diner favorite, the mighty Caesar. Both have been essential parts of road trips, sweet summer memories, and lazy Sundays. When Jonathan and I first moved Bittered Sling up to the Okanagan Valley in 2014, we'd spend six to seven hours in the car driving up from Vancouver, and then have the same journey back. Nothing but the road and countryside ahead, with good company, a killer playlist, and a double-toasted everything bagel with cream cheese, tomato, and cucumber from Tims, along with a double-double coffee. There's no coffee in this drink (that would be weird), but the sentiment is there—we always end up finding a Tim Hortons when we're out of gas, out of food, and in need of a stretch. So in this homage to Canada's other iconic drink, the Caesar, I've taken part of my standard Tims order and incorporated it here with the Bagel Shrub and Everything Bagel Spice. Most people outside Canada cannot understand why you'd drink a Caesar (which is made of tomato juice, clam juice, and spices), while most people *in* Canada think making one involves opening a bottle of premix and dumping it into a glass with three cubes of ice, herbs, and vodka. But like any great cocktail, it's the ritual of how you make it, how you garnish it, and how the guest receives the drink that matters. I learned the proper technique to making tomato-and-vodka-based drinks properly in 2000, with the roll technique (later the throw) an essential part of the process to ensure that the dilution and chill are just right, without aeration. The spices are personal; I don't automatically use celery salt, Tabasco, and Worcestershire; instead, I choose based on my mood and the cuisine style. To be honest, it's a difficult cocktail to mess up. So without further ado, here is my ode to Canada's quintessential drinks—the Double-Double Caesar.

Serves 1

Area of inspiration: Crowsnest Highway (Hwy 5), British Columbia
Inspired by: the Caesar

—

1½ ounces (45 mL) vodka

6 ounces (175 mL) Denman Street Caesar Mix (page 157)

¼ ounce (7.5 mL) Bagel Shrub (page 156)

3 dashes aromatic bitters (like Bittered Sling Kensington)

2 dashes Tabasco sauce (optional)

Pinch kosher salt

Pinch cracked black pepper

Rim and Garnish: Lemon juice and Everything Bagel Spice (page 157); double-toasted bagel cracker, cream cheese, black pepper, poppy seeds, sesame seeds

Method

Rim a Collins glass with lemon juice and Everything Bagel Spice and set aside. To a shaker filled with cubed ice, add the vodka, Caesar mix, shrub, bitters, Tabasco sauce (if using), salt, and pepper. Place a Hawthorne strainer over the shaker and strain into an empty shaker. Strain back into the shaker with the ice. Transferring the cocktail back and forth allows the drink to chill in one shaker, while the other shaker mixes it without too much dilution or aeration. Do this for about 15 seconds. Strain one last time into the prepared Collins glass and top with cubed ice. For the garnish, spread the cracker with cream cheese and top with black pepper, poppy seeds, and sesame seeds.

Estonian Finnisher

If you have family history in Eastern Europe as I do, then a trip to this area can be seen almost as a rite of passage. As a Canadian, I'm always trying to delve into my heritage, especially regarding when my ancestors came across the pond to start a new life here in North America. As the administrator of our family tree since 2003, I have uncovered so many treasures. One of the biggest discoveries was that my ancestors on my paternal side and Jonathan's family all come from Eastern Europe as far back as I can research (the 1600s). So traveling to that region was a dream come true. Riga, Latvia, was stunning. The historical district was filled with old landmarks woven into modern buildings. We had dinner across from the Riga Cathedral, built in the thirteenth century and the largest medieval church in the region. In Lithuania, a group of bartenders showed me a bit of the nightlife. In Vilnius's old city, dozens of cool cocktail bars lined the streets, focused on their reimagined versions of classic cocktails. The region marches to the beat of its own drum. The best of the best introduces excited guests to the world of cocktails their way—my favorite way to discover a city. I expected my last stop, Tallinn, Estonia, to be similar to Riga and Vilnius, but I was in for a treat. At the northern tip of the city, travelers can take a two-hour ferry across the Baltic Sea to Helsinki, Finland, so I wondered whether the food and beverages would be influenced more by Nordic or Eastern European traditions. Tallinn was the best of both worlds, offering some of the best bread, fish, vegetables, and light cocktails I've had anywhere. It was so unexpected. The mouthwatering drinks were all less-is-more, light-handed preparations with a high acid content. My "hop" around the Baltics lasted five days and wouldn't have been possible without the help of some great people. I hope everyone has a chance to see these cities with the help of excellent local guides.

Serves 1

Area of inspiration: the Baltics
Inspired by: the Highball

———

1 ounce (30 mL) vodka

½ ounce (15 mL) quince eau de vie

2 ounces (60 mL) Apple Honey Shrub (page 156)

2 dashes celery bitters
(like Bittered Sling Cascade Celery)

3 ounces (90 mL) kombucha or kvass

Garnish and Sides: Fresh mint and rosemary, fresh edible flower (optional), lemon wheel, black bread, whipped butter, kosher salt, fennel pollen

Method

To a Collins glass filled with cubed ice, add the vodka, eau de vie, shrub, and bitters. Stir gently with a bar spoon to chill. Add more ice if necessary; it should be right to the top. Fill the glass with kombucha and stir just to combine. For the garnish, thread the mint, rosemary, and flower (if using) through the center of the lemon wheel. Spread a slice of black bread with butter and sprinkle with salt and fennel pollen. Serve on the side.

Georgia on My Mind

We aren't talking about the southern United States, but about the Georgia in Eastern Europe, well known for its delicious food and beverages. My friend Katya in Kyiv, Ukraine, always tells me about the great ingredients and foods that she and her husband have discovered in many trips to Georgia. Each time I visit Katya, she takes me to a traditional Ukrainian restaurant and a traditional Georgian restaurant. My dad's family comes from Eastern Europe, but they've been settled in Canada for three generations, and it hasn't been possible to research and discover the food of our ancestors there. Luckily, Katya is an excellent tour guide. She says Georgia is one of the very few ex-Soviet nations that has kept their traditional foods and dishes alive. The Georgia on My Mind showcases these Eastern European cultures and celebrates the stone fruits that grow so well in the region. The secret to this drink is the Rainbow Beet Cordial—a combination of beets, vanilla, pink and white peppercorns, hibiscus, raspberries, and coconut. Beets are commonly associated with Eastern European cuisine and tend to be used in savory dishes. This is one of the most remarkable applications, and once the cordial is made, you can store it in the fridge and use it in other cocktails with a sour base, in smoothies, or in steamed milk for a "pink latte."

Method

To a shaker filled with cubed ice, add the vodka, eau de vie, cordial, bitters, and egg white. Using some force, shake hard for 10 seconds. Using a small fine-mesh bar sieve to catch the loose ice chips, double strain into a cocktail glass or coupe. Sprinkle pepper on top and garnish with a beet chip.

Serves 1

Area of inspiration: Georgia via Ukraine
Inspired by: the Vodka Sour

———

1½ ounces (45 mL) vodka

½ ounce (15 mL) Mirabelle plum eau de vie

1 ounce (30 mL) Rainbow Beet Cordial (page 159)

1 dash cherry bitters
(like Bittered Sling Suius Cherry)

1 egg white (optional, see note)

Garnish: Ground pink peppercorns, Dehydrated Sweet Beet Chip (recipe follows)

Dehydrated Sweet Beet Chips
Carefully using a mandoline, thinly slice a candy cane beet. Place superfine or granulated sugar on a shallow plate and spread it out flat. Coat both sides of each beet slice in sugar and place on parchment paper. Dry in a dehydrator or a 200°F (93°C) oven overnight. Let cool, then store in a paper towel–lined airtight container for up to 7 days and use as garnish.

Note: If you are concerned about the food safety of raw eggs, use 1 ounce (30 mL) pasteurized liquid egg whites in place of the egg white.

Grand Palace

What I love most about Thailand is the Thai bartenders' and chefs' understanding of flavor, which seems to come naturally. Their ability to achieve balance in their traditional cooking style is a marvel and makes a lot of dishes I've had in other places seem rather... bland. Not only are the dishes memorable, but the flavors deepen over time too. After I touched down in Bangkok with a group of bartenders, we were hosted for a dinner of family-style food at a small restaurant specializing in traditional Thai dishes and drinks. You can learn a lot about a culture, people, and ingredients by listening to the dish origins and tasting alongside. We were sweating profusely from the chilies and salivating from the acidity, and our mouths were dancing from the spices, fish sauce, and fruits we consumed that evening. The next day, we made our way over to the Bamboo Bar. This famed bar opened in 1940 and is situated inside the historic Mandarin Oriental Hotel, perched on the edge of the Chao Phraya River. It feels like walking through history, or a period piece on the silver screen. The hotel has hosted many famous writers, from Ernest Hemingway to Graham Greene. As bartenders and creators, we often turn to writing for inspiration when it comes to the gift of the gab we're known for. One of my favorite shops in Bangkok is at duty-free (that must sound crazy), so before our flight, I stopped at the dried fruit emporium in the airport, which sells tropical fruits dried and packed for international travel. The number of fruits is endless, but I'm always after the passion fruit and coconut. Without question, the passion fruit powder is the secret to this marvelous cocktail that truly captures the essence of my trip. To me, this drink will always be linked to my happy memories of great friends in Thailand like Mr. Ball and Jamie Rhind.

Serves 1

Area of inspiration: Bangkok, Thailand
Inspired by: the Daisy

———

Freeze-dried passion fruit powder (available online)

1½ ounces (45 mL) vodka

½ ounce (15 mL) coconut liqueur

1 ounce (30 mL) fresh lemon juice

1 ounce (30 mL) Vanilla Syrup (page 159)

2 dashes chocolate bitters
(like Bittered Sling Malagasy Chocolate)

1 egg white (see note)

Garnish: 4 drops aromatic bitters

Method
Dust the outside of a frozen coupe glass with passion fruit powder. To a shaker, add the vodka, liqueur, lemon juice, syrup, chocolate bitters, and egg white. Dry shake (without ice) for 5 seconds to emulsify the ingredients. Open the shaker and add cubed ice. Using some force, shake hard for 5 seconds. Using a small fine-mesh bar sieve to catch the loose ice chips, double strain into the glass. For the garnish, add 4 drops of angostura bitters on top. Using a toothpick, drag each dot into the center.

Note: If you are concerned about the food safety of raw eggs, use 1 ounce (30 mL) pasteurized liquid egg whites in place of the egg white.

Here Comes the Sun

One of my biggest dreams was to visit India, and I couldn't believe it when I was finally boarding the plane to do just that. My friend Prerana Sitaraman arranged an amazing schedule for us, visiting bartenders across three cities in six days—how ambitious! I landed in Bangalore late at night. The air stood still; it was hot and humid, with the palm trees outside the airport swaying gently. The next morning, I could hear the faint sound of monkeys in the neighboring park—what an alarm clock! One of the ambassadors I met, Zack, mentioned that the monkeys entered through an open window in his apartment and broke his iPhone. Prerana met me in the lobby and took me to eat ghee dosas with coconut chutney, fresh mint, and cilantro at an outdoor market. After lunch, we walked through the market, the strong scent of fresh marigold flowers filling our noses. Prerana told me that "the marigold is originally Mexican and was brought to India (along with chilies) about 350 to 400 years ago. It's used a lot as offerings at festivals and during weddings. Apart from their odor acting as an insect repellent, their fragrance is wonderful and symbolizes the sun and, hence, positivity and energy." This drink is a lovely expression of sunny ingredients, in the form of a long, refreshing Collins, with the stunning aroma and texture (yes, you can eat them!) of the marigolds on top.

Method

Add cubed ice to a Lewis bag and smash into chips with a mallet. Fill a wineglass (tall or stemless) carefully with cubed ice and add the vodka, vermouth, cordial, marmalade, and bitters. Stir gently with a bar spoon to chill. Top with carbonated water as needed and stir just to combine. For the garnish, use a peeler to remove a nice piece of peel from a washed lemon. Using a paring knife, trim the edges on all sides. Twist the peel to express the oil over the cocktail, then drop it into the glass. Add the flowers and serve.

Serves 1

Area of inspiration: Bangalore, India
Inspired by: the Collins

———

1 ounce (30 mL) vodka

1 ounce (30 mL) Solar Flare Orange Vermouth (page 239) or Cinzano Orancio vermouth

¾ ounce (22.5 mL) All-Purpose Cordial (page 232)

1 bar spoon orange or ginger marmalade

1 dash grapefruit bitters (like Bittered Sling Grapefruit & Hops)

Chilled carbonated water, as needed

Garnish: Lemon twist, fresh edible marigold flowers

SIX DAYS IN INDIA

After spending some time in Bangalore, complete with southern Indian rain-forest-like weather, Prerana and I met up with some friends and spent a night with bartenders and other great folks in Mumbai, a place I had always longed to visit. Mumbai was busy and, being right on the ocean, incredibly humid. It rained every sixty minutes—I had arrived smack in the middle of monsoon season. Prerana and I dined at local joints that celebrated the flavors and ingredients of the region, and met with bartenders who brought the same unique flavors to life in their drinks.

After our twenty-hour trip to Mumbai, we were off again to New Delhi, our last stop. The India finals for a bartending competition were being held in a hotel complex close to the airport. This was a smart choice; it felt like it might take a lifetime to cross to the other side of the vast city. On a break between sessions, I asked some of the local team if there was a place to buy light linen clothing, shoes, and spices—all very important to bring back from my first trip to India. Our local ambassador brought us to a spice shop not far from the hotel. Outside the shop, an older gentleman sat guarding the spice grinder. Inside, the smell was overpowering. As a bitters maker, I am really connected to the flavor of spices; in fact, one of my favorite things to do is eat whole spices and let the flavors take over my palate. I sampled one spice after the other—green cardamom pods, cinnamon, peppercorns, you name

it—breaking them, examining them, closing my eyes while capturing the aroma, and finally eating them.

After we left the spice shop, we headed to a local market specializing in clothing and shoes. By this time, the sun was setting and the heat was becoming more manageable. The temperature was still 107.6°F (42°C), but that was down from 116.6°F (47°C) earlier in the day, when my shoes were literally melting to the pavement. Unbelievable! I still wear the array of colorful light linen outfits I bought when it's super-hot in the summer months, and they always remind me of this amazing experience.

Prerana and the ambassador team are such kind, wonderful souls, and I hope one day to visit them again. Six days in India wasn't nearly enough, but we sure did pack a lot in to make it memorable.

Seven Mile Mule

Grand Cayman has some of the most beautiful water to dip your toes in. Though I was lucky enough to have been there a few times before, one of my favorite trips was in 2019, when I was invited by former Ritz beverage director Amba Lamb to attend the Cayman Cookout as a guest and presenter. Working closely with the island's bartending community was the goal, where we trained and developed the local programs and spent time with folks who were just as excited about drinks as we were. During the happy hour break, I was in the sea with Dennis Tamse, a long-time friend and a great bartender from the Netherlands. Dennis and I met in Chicago in 2015 at a bartending competition in Chicago. As we floated out into the sea, we turned and looked back at the shore. The sand was shimmering along Seven Mile Beach, and we could hear kids playing at neighboring resorts and music blasting from the Ritz patio. Dennis turned to me and said, "Not bad for a couple of bartenders." We had our 4:30 p.m. meeting in the sea for the remainder of the trip, chatting about life, our families, and our jobs. It's good to have friends who keep you honest and present. We often forget to stop and appreciate the moment, and the journey each of us has taken to get here.

Method

To a shaker filled with cubed ice, add the vodka, sherry, cordial, and bitters. Using some force, shake hard for 5 seconds. Using a Hawthorne strainer, strain into a Collins glass. Top with the ginger beer and stir just to combine. Garnish with the pomelo peel and mint.

Serves 1

Area of inspiration: Grand Cayman
Inspired by: the Moscow Mule

———

1 ounce (30 mL) vodka

½ ounce (15 mL) fino sherry

1 ounce (30 mL) Pomelo Cordial (page 158)

2 dashes grapefruit bitters
(like Bittered Sling Grapefruit & Hops)

3 ounces (90 mL) chilled ginger beer

Garnish: Pomelo or grapefruit peel, fresh mint sprig

Wanna-Bee

At Okanagan Valley's Tantalus Vineyards, nestled in the foothills above Kelowna, British Columbia, the wine-maker might reign supreme, but the honeybees in the apiary rule the land. One brisk morning in wine country, we toured endless rows of Riesling, Chardonnay, and Pinot Noir grapes. As a sommelier, I'm always interested in learning more about grapes and how they thrive in varying terroirs. I was once stung in the face by a bee while rollerblading to work (do people still rollerblade?), so I remember needing to overcome my fear that day, but eventually I embraced the bees like I was Briar Rose dancing and singing through the forest in *Sleeping Beauty*. The wine, the vineyard, and the apiary will always hold a place in my heart. It's where I was first inspired to use wine in cocktails, and I now use great Okanagan bottles to make vermouths and aromatized wines from scratch. Tantalus Vineyards is also where I fully realized the power and potential of bees and the necessity of protecting their habitat. Wines with different intensity in flavor, body, and character will add something unique to the finished modifier, and that's apparent in the different countries where I have made this drink. This style of drink wants to be somewhere between the classic martini, and martinez—a beautiful recipe design you'll see throughout this book. I was thrilled to feature this drink and its story on the menu at the two-Michelin-star restaurant the Greenhouse in Dublin, Ireland, where I worked with my good friend, Chef Mark Moriarty, to bring this to life.

Method

Fill a mixing glass with cubed ice. Add the vodka, sherry, cordial, bitters, and saline solution. Stir with a bar spoon for 20 rotations (this ensures optimal dilution and temperature). Using a julep strainer, strain into a chilled Nick and Nora glass or coupette. For the garnish, use a peeler to remove a nice piece of peel from a washed lemon. Twist the peel to express the oil over the cocktail, then discard. Garnish with a single marigold on top (or use whatever is stunning and in season).

Serves 1

Area of inspiration: Okanagan Valley, Canada
Inspired by: the Martini and the Martinez

———

2 ounces (60 mL) vodka

¾ ounce (22.5 mL) Marigold Wine (page 157)

¼ ounce (7.5 mL) All-Purpose Flower Cordial (page 46)

2 dashes grapefruit bitters
(like Bittered Sling Grapefruit & Hops)

1 dash Saline Solution (page 95)

Garnish: Lemon oil, edible marigold flower

We're Pickle People

I talk a lot about my family heritage in this book, and rightly so. My outlook on food and drinks was bred as much through experiences in my childhood as through learned experiences from my adult years. My bubie Rose, who's 103 years old, has been telling me the same story since she was in her seventies: "You know, my father's family made pickles in Poland, and my cousin makes the best honey mustard. It's out of this world," she'd say. She always joked that her father, Moishe, along with most of his brothers and sisters, came to Canada in a pickle barrel in the late 1800s. There's harsh truth to that—they wanted to leave Poland, no matter how. My bubie and I work as often as we can on the family tree, trying to capture all the stories and the people in the extended Gollom/Oppenheim/Grafstein family. Despite her culinary origins in the pickle business, Bubie Rose wasn't an avid cook. She was busy running her father's fabric and textile shops in the 1940s. When she started taking a greater role in our lives as our bubie, we had a choice: eat like her or make your own arrangements. That meant kosher meals, boxes of Manischewitz "something," flax bagels, cream cheese, lox, chopped chicken liver (for my brothers), Honeycup Mustard (made by another one of her cousins), and jar after jar of pickles. Bubie Rose's famous line was: "Finish it. At home you can diet. Here you can eat everything." Throughout the years, we tried to get Bubie Rose out of the house more for meals beyond the bagel depot and coffee shops. She was always twitchy about spending money in restaurants, as she thought the food at home would be better and cost half the price. As it turns out, she's the matriarch of four legendary bakers, two bartenders, and multiple business owners—all in hospitality, food, and beverage. The name of this drink, We're Pickle People, relates to her stories; there were never just yes or no answers to our questions about life and business. Bubie Rose shared her times of struggle and success to paint a broader picture of her path, to help us figure out our way. They were stories meant to inspire, about a family that started with nothing, worked 24/7 for the small wins, and survived to pass down their knowledge.

Serves 1

Area of inspiration: Poland
Inspired by: the Corpse Reviver #2

———

1 ounce (30 mL) vodka

1 ounce (30 mL) aquavit

1 ounce (30 mL) Honey Cup Shrub (page 158)

1 ounce (30 mL) sour pickle brine
(from kosher dills)

2 dashes orange bitters
(like Bittered Sling Orange & Juniper)

Garnish: Long dill pickle spear, fresh dill sprig

Method

To a shaker filled with cubed ice, add the vodka, aquavit, shrub, pickle brine, and bitters. Using some force, shake hard for 5 seconds. Using a Hawthorne strainer, strain into a highball glass filled with cubed ice. Garnish with the pickle spear and dill.

Mise en Place Recipes

Bagel Shrub

Makes 12 ounces (375 mL)

½ ounce (15 mL) olive oil

2 bay leaves

2 cloves garlic, minced

1 shallot, thinly sliced

5 grams sesame seeds

5 grams poppy seeds

1 gram salt

1 gram freshly cracked black pepper

15 grams plain bagel, toasted and chopped into pieces

8 ounces (250 mL) cane vinegar

4 ounces (125 mL) filtered water

2 ounces (60 mL) fresh lemon juice

1 ounce (30 mL) Simple Syrup (page 47)

In a small saucepan, heat the oil over low heat. Add the bay leaves, garlic, shallot, sesame seeds, poppy seeds, salt, and pepper, and cook, stirring, until aromatic. Add the bagel, vinegar, water, lemon, and syrup, and bring to a simmer. Simmer for 5 minutes, or until fragrant. Remove from the heat and let stand for 30 minutes. Strain the liquid through a mesh sieve, then through cheesecloth to microfilter. Store in a sanitized bottle, labeled with the date, in the fridge for up to 10 days.

Apple Honey Shrub

Makes 16 ounces (500 mL)

200 grams honey

7 ounces (200 mL) freshly pressed apple juice (strained is fine)

3½ ounces (100 mL) cane vinegar

To a blender, add the honey, apple juice, and vinegar. Blend on medium until the honey is dissolved. Strain through a mesh sieve into a sanitized bottle, label with the date, and store in the fridge for up to 10 days.

Denman Street Caesar Mix

Makes 1¼ quarts (1.25 L), vegan recipe

1 can (28 ounces/796 mL) peeled whole San Marzano tomatoes

1 small dried ancho chili (see note)

100 grams carrot, chopped

100 grams unpeeled cucumber, chopped

100 grams celery, chopped

2 grams kosher salt

2 grams freshly ground black pepper

1 gram yellow mustard seeds

1 gram fenugreek seeds

1 gram ground sumac

1 gram smoked paprika (mild or hot)

2 ounces (60 mL) fresh lemon juice

½ ounce (15 mL) Simple Syrup (page 47)

⅓ ounce (10 mL) soy sauce (preferably white)

Add all ingredients to a blender and blend on medium-high for 30 seconds or until smooth. Strain through a mesh strainer to catch any remaining big pieces. Clean the strainer and repeat if necessary. Store in a sanitized bottle, labeled with the date, in the fridge for up to 10 days. Shake or stir before using.

Note: If you're sensitive to chili heat, omit the ancho pepper. If using it, make sure you wear a glove to handle it, and keep your hands away from your eyes.

Everything Bagel Spice

Makes 215 grams

125 grams sesame seeds

60 grams poppy seeds

5 grams fennel seeds

2.5 grams caraway seeds

15 grams nutritional yeast

2 grams garlic powder

2 grams onion powder

2 grams celery salt

1 gram hot chili flakes

1 gram citric acid

In a dry skillet, toast the sesame, poppy, fennel, and caraway seeds for 2 minutes or until aromatic. Using a mortar and pestle, crush the toasted seeds. Add the remaining ingredients and crush together to combine. Store in a small jar, labeled with the date, in the pantry for up to 1 month.

———

Marigold Wine

Makes 16 ounces (500 mL), 15% ABV

10 grams fresh edible marigold flowers

8 ounces (250 mL) fino sherry

8 ounces (250 mL) dry pinot gris white wine

Add the flowers, sherry, and wine to a 16-ounce (500 mL) jar. Fold a paper coffee filter in half and place on top of the flowers, pressing to soak, to keep the flowers submerged and moist. Cover and infuse for 24 hours in the fridge. Strain the liquid into a sanitized bottle, pressing out liquid from the flowers. Label the bottle with the date and ABV. Store in the fridge for up to 10 days.

Honey Cup Shrub

Makes 10 ounces (300 mL)

120 grams creamed raw white honey

4 ounces (125 mL) filtered water

2 ounces (60 mL) cane vinegar

5 grams yellow mustard seeds

1 gram ground turmeric

1 gram ground horseradish

1 gram salt

Using an immersion circulator, bring a pot of water to 195°F (90°C) (or use a stem thermometer to hold the temperature on medium-high heat). In a bowl, whisk together the honey, water, and vinegar until the honey is dissolved. Add the mustard seeds, turmeric, horseradish, and salt to a heatproof food-safe bag and top with the honey water. Remove the air from the bag, seal, and clip it to the side of the pot, ensuring that the mixture is underwater. Cook for 1½ hours. Transfer the bag to an ice bath and let cool. Strain the liquid into a sanitized bottle, label with the date, and store in the fridge for up to 10 days.

Pomelo Cordial

Makes 10 ounces (300 mL)

200 grams superfine or granulated sugar

10 grams citric acid

7 ounces (200 mL) filtered water

100 grams pomelo peels

100 grams pomelo segments (thick white pith removed), chopped

Using an immersion circulator, bring a pot of water to 195°F (90°C) (or use a stem thermometer to hold the temperature on medium-high heat). In a bowl, whisk together the sugar, citric acid, and water until the sugar is dissolved. Add the pomelo peels and segments to a heatproof food-safe bag and top with the sugar water. Remove the air from the bag, seal, and clip it to the side of the pot, ensuring that the mixture is underwater. Cook for 1½ hours. Transfer the bag to an ice bath and let cool. Strain the liquid into a sanitized bottle, label with the date, and store in the fridge for up to 10 days.

Rainbow Beet Cordial

Makes 16 ounces (500 mL)

1 large yellow beet, refrigerated before use

1 large rainbow beet, refrigerated before use

7 grams citric acid

7 grams tartaric acid

2 grams whole pink peppercorns

0.5 gram whole white peppercorns

2 grams dried hibiscus flowers

20 grams dried raspberries

1 teaspoon (5 mL) vanilla extract

Pinch fine pink salt

300 grams superfine or granulated sugar

Set up a juicer. Peel and chop the beets into small pieces. Add the citric and tartaric acids to the bottom of a small pitcher and use that to catch the juice. (This prevents the juice from browning.) Run the beet pieces through the juicer. Stir the juice to dissolve the acids, then strain into a blender and add the peppercorns, hibiscus flowers, raspberries, vanilla, salt, and sugar. Blend on medium until the sugar is dissolved. Strain the liquid through cheesecloth to microfilter. This syrup should be vibrant. Store in a sanitized bottle, labeled with the date, in the fridge for up to 10 days.

Note: Beets oxidize more slowly if they've been in the fridge.

Vanilla Syrup

Makes 16 ounces (500 mL)

300 grams superfine or granulated sugar

7 ounces (200 mL) filtered water

½ vanilla bean

Using an immersion circulator, bring a pot of water to 195°F (90°C) (or use a stem thermometer to hold the temperature on medium-high heat). In a bowl, whisk together the sugar and water until the sugar is dissolved. Split the vanilla bean and scrape out the seeds, reserving the bean to make vanilla extract (see note, page 132). Add the vanilla seeds to a heatproof food-safe bag and top with the sugar water. Remove the air from the bag, seal, and clip it to the side of the pot, ensuring that the mixture is underwater. Cook for 1½ hours. Transfer the bag to an ice bath and let cool. Strain the liquid into a sanitized bottle, label with the date, and store in the fridge for up to 10 days.

Whiskey

Chicka Cherry Cola

My friend Angie Poirier is one of the hardest-working women in the drinks business, supporting outstanding programs for local bars in Vancouver and right across British Columbia. Angie was also one of the early brand partners in Kale & Nori's programs, back when Jonathan and I were just starting out in 2010. She started calling me "wifey" back in 2014, and our relationship evolved even further later that summer when Angie brought me to Scotland to learn more about the distilleries and whiskies I had been working with for years, at UVA and Kale & Nori. At that point, I hadn't done much traveling outside Canada. We landed in Aberdeen and drove from there to Inverness, the heart of the Scottish Highlands, touring many distilleries and discovering delicious drams along the way. The big standouts were Orkney Island in the far north, and the island of Islay in the west. Islay was really special—our timing was perfect and in our 24 hours there, we attended a huge island wedding that happened to be underway. The party was built out in a field under perfect moonlight, with a makeshift bar and dance floor under a tent. The bonfires made from wooden skids illuminated the bar, which was filled with whisky from near and far, a ton of bourbon, and every fizzy mixer you could dream of, from the bright-orange Iron-Bru to cherry Coke. Our team of amazing spirits buyers and bartenders from across Canada couldn't believe the fun, or the surreal moment of our timing. Even the sheep were excited! Our flight was early the next day—we didn't sleep much. Thanks to Angie, those memories forged in Scotland remain part of my story-telling repertoire today, and drastically change the flavor and feeling of scotch whisky for me.

Method

In a container, combine the bourbon, vermouth, water, cordial, and bitters. Add to a carbonated drink maker (like the Drinkmate) and follow the manufacturer's instructions to carbonate. Gently release the pressure and pour into a Collins glass filled with cubed ice. Garnish with the lime wedge.

Serves 1

Area of inspiration: Islay, Scotland
Inspired by: the Cuba Libre

———

¾ ounce (22.5 mL) bourbon

¾ ounce (22.5 mL) Nebula Pink Vermouth (page 238) or Cocchi Rosa wine

4 ounces (125 mL) cold filtered water

1 ounce (30 mL) Cherry Cola Cordial (page 184)

1 dash aromatic bitters
(like Bittered Sling Plum & Rootbeer)

Garnish: Lime wedge

THE MAGIC OF ISLAY

For the average traveler, Islay—the southernmost island of Scotland's Inner Hebrides—might seem like an unexpected layover, but for the whisky lover, romance seeker, and bon vivant, it's nothing short of breathtaking. It captured my heart at first sight, despite heavy rain blowing sideways under my umbrella as we disembarked from the plane. But nothing could prepare me for what followed: nestled among thousands of sheep, the ruins of Viking inhabitants and Norse gods stand shoulder to shoulder with some of the greatest whisky distilleries, where smoke reigns supreme, peat is the terroir, and the dram is queen.

Traveling down a narrow road toward the town of Port Ellen, we passed fields of bright-yellow flowers, green meadows, and mobs of sheep. Our driver pointed out the Laphroaig peat field, and we raced to one side of the bus to snap pictures. After eight days in Scotland, this was the pièce de résistance—the world of Islay as we were meant to experience it. This trip changed my life and the way I looked at Islay whiskies. It's also where I met John Campbell, the "Prince of Whisky," and my good friend and the longtime distillery manager for Laphroaig (in 2021, John left Islay to help develop the Lochlea Distillery on the west coast of Scotland's mainland).

Romance is what connects us to products. We can smell, sip, and savor ingredients that transport us to a certain time and place and develop a bond that cannot be broken. Few people have the opportunity to grab a handful of barley from the malting floor, stand inside a 2,000-square-foot kiln, have a private tasting with the master distiller, dig through the peat fields in wellies, or plant a flag claiming a square foot of Islay's landscape as your lifelong lease. Several distilleries call Islay home, and I'm thrilled to have had a chance to experience most of them. From Caol Ila to Lagavulin, Bowmore to Ardbeg, Bruichladdich to Laphroaig, the whiskies are special, and the people behind them for centuries are even more so.

As I walked along the beach just beyond the Kildalton distilleries on the south coast eating raw broccoli from a Tesco Express bag, catching a glimpse of Ireland in the distance, stepping over bull kelp and moss, and taking in the sea air, I realized that this was one of the most magical places on earth.

I'll drink to that.

Kentucky Crush

Back in 2012, Angie Poirier and Jeff Meyers from Beam Suntory were the first to sponsor Bittered Sling Bistro, a pop-restaurant we owned for 5 years in Vancouver. The idea was to create a theme each month, find a sponsor who made sense, and invite creative bartenders to develop a thoughtful beverage presentation, featuring Bittered Sling bitters, to match Chef Jonathan's dishes (cooked to the same theme). I would always create the apéritif for folks as they walked into Legacy Liquor Store (our Vancouver pop-up venue) and back to the forty-two-person harvest table. Legacy had an open kitchen, and it was the perfect setting for our program. Over the coming years, dozens of bartenders, including Justin Taylor and Gerry Jobe, both of whom we designed custom bitters for, would participate in the program—the who's who of bar talent—but Jay Jones, a legendary Vancouver bartender, launched the program as the first guest presenter. The theme was Amusement Park, so the food was fun, colorful, and delicious, and the drinks were equally exciting. In 2014, Angie and Jeff rewarded us for the hard work on Bittered Sling Bistro with a trip to Kentucky to learn more about bourbon, the industry, and the key locations that bring the category to life. Jeff, Jay, Jonathan, and I spent four days with the horses at Churchill Downs, the many great bars and restaurants in Louisville, and half a dozen distilleries, an experience that would keep us excited about the possibilities of regional foods and beverages for years to come. Having spent many years as an ambassador myself, I know the power of sharing with bartenders and paying it forward to ensure they have opportunities to learn on location, as we did. This drink is a perfect apéritif and brings the flavors we commonly associate with bourbon together into a crushable format.

Serves 1

Area of inspiration: Louisville, Kentucky
Inspired by: the Sweet Tea Highball

——

1 ounce (30 mL) bourbon

1 ounce (30 mL) Solar Flare Orange Vermouth (page 239) or Cinzano Orancio vermouth

1 ounce (30 mL) Jaffa Orange Crush Cordial (page 185)

2 dashes peach bitters
(like Bittered Sling Clingstone Peach)

4 ounces (125 mL) chilled peach-flavored black tea

Garnish: Peach fan

Method

To a Collins glass filled with cubed ice, add the bourbon, vermouth, cordial, and bitters. Stir gently with a bar spoon to chill. Add more ice if necessary; it should be right to the top. Fill the glass with tea and stir just to combine. For the garnish, slice a long cheek off the side of a peach. Cut it into 5 thin slices (1/16 inch/2 mm thick) and thread a cocktail pick through the bottom edge of all the slices together. Fan out from the top once the bottom is secure, and place the pick side down into the glass.

One Below

For over a decade, big competitions such as Bacardi Legacy, Patron Perfectionists, World Class, Beefeater MIXLDN, and the Bombay Sapphire Most Imaginative Bartender programs, have played a critical role in developing education, networking, and opportunities for Canadian bartenders. Since those early days, some incredible bartenders have trained and developed through regional, national, and global programs, helping shape Canada's top tier industry, while maintaining accessibility for new generations of bartenders rising to the occasion. In Canada, Michael Armistead, a longtime colleague and now a good friend, leads World Class. He's been one of the main reasons that Canadian bartenders have had these opportunities; he's created annual education and competition programming for bartenders at every level. After almost a decade in Canada, Michael's leadership in the program has brought us closer to our American brothers and sisters (after two years of blended Canada and US finals) and set up Canada's annual entrance to the world stage. It takes a village to make great things happen, but it takes a visionary to keep the village thriving year after year. Michael is a consummate host, someone who looks after people and who loves to welcome bartenders, whether from Canada or other countries. My homage to Michael is inspired by the old fashioned, which is in his top four along with tequila, a gibson, and champoo (champagne). The name comes from Michael's basement bar in Georgian Bay, where he and his partner, Wayne, host us any chance they get. We refer to those moments as "the good life," or simply using the hashtag #noscrubs2017. From time spent in a basement bar, to fancy dinners, and carpool karaoke, Michael's company is simply the best.

Serves 1

Area of inspiration: Georgian Bay, Canada
Inspired by: the Old Fashioned

———

2 ounces (60 mL) Canadian 100% rye whisky

½ ounce (15 mL) Islay whisky

½ ounce (15 mL) maple syrup

2 dashes chocolate bitters
(like Bittered Sling Malagasy Chocolate)

Garnish: Orange twist, lemon twist, brandied cherry

Method

Fill a mixing glass with cubed ice. Add the rye whisky, Islay whisky, maple syrup, and bitters. Stir with a bar spoon for 15 to 20 rotations. Using a julep strainer, strain over a large ice cube in an old-fashioned glass. For the garnish, use a peeler to remove a nice piece of peel from a washed orange, and one from a washed lemon. Using a paring knife, trim the edges of both peels on all sides. Roll the lemon peel tightly into a cylinder, and thread on to the pick. Add the brandied cherry, then repeat the rolling process with the orange peel. Place the pick in the glass.

Polar Vortex

There are a few things Canadians tend to share with the world: our love for Tim Hortons coffee, road tripping, cottages, and rye whisky. You'll often hear us talking about the country's variable terrain, from the mountains in the west to the prairies to the Canadian Shield of solid rock to the Maritime islands in the Atlantic. But we rarely mention the Arctic winds and subzero temperatures, or how we cope with them. Cocktails are an excellent place to start—a wee nip to keep you warm. In the center of the country stands one of Canada's coldest places: the province of Manitoba. During one January visit, an icy Arctic airflow blessed a group of West Coast bartenders with frigid temperatures of −77.8°F (−61°C). You cannot imagine the feeling of your nostrils and legs freezing in seconds despite your floor-length puffy coat, toque, and other winter gear. Our friends from bars and restaurants across Winnipeg are no strangers to this weather, and looking after tourists who are not accustomed to the polar chill is part of their hospitality. They welcome folks by the dozens to visit their venues with working heaters, open arms, hot food, and delicious drinks, not to mention the smiles and laughs that make us feel like we're complaining about the weather for no reason. They take a couple of light-hearted jabs, suggesting that people from Vancouver can't handle really cold weather, and they're probably right. This cocktail tastes like Canada in a glass, from the warmth of diverse friendships to the icy-cold temperatures in the peak of winter's wrath in central Canada.

Serves 1

Area of inspiration: Winnipeg, Manitoba
Inspired by: the Whisky Sour

———

1½ ounces (45 mL) Canadian 100% rye whisky

2 ounces (60 mL) Apple Honey Shrub (page 156)

2 dashes lemon bitters
(like Bittered Sling Lem-Marrakech)

Garnish: Evergreen wreath, Balsam Fir Spray
(page 184)

Method

Wrap a highball glass with an evergreen wreath, affixing it to the glass with butcher's twine or a rubber band. Spray the inside of the glass with balsam spray, then fill the glass with cubed ice. To a shaker filled with cubed ice, add the whisky, shrub, and bitters. Using some force, shake hard for 5 seconds. Using a small fine-mesh bar sieve to catch the loose ice chips, double strain into the prepared glass. Finish with another spray of the balsam spray.

The Unclimbable

This is a low-proof beverage, perfect for writing and reflection. Speaking of reflection, a few years ago, during an interview, I was asked, "What did you want to be when you grew up? What did you aspire to?" My answer from my later childhood years was always the same: "Go to law school." But I also remember being seven years old and writing: "When I grow up, I want to be a mountain climber." Whether physically or metaphorically, I've always been fascinated by the "unachievable" and "impossible." In fact, over the years, I've developed a real fascination with mountains and a deeper connection to the earth, believing that even the unclimbable heights looming above can be conquered. I'm not sure if I'll ever live out my dream of scaling the walls of the Mackenzie Mountains, but I'm happy to gaze at them and reflect on my own world, and how I've scaled other mountains that have challenged me in a different way. In 2017, I wrote a program of cocktails and stories inspired by these majestic earthly structures called "The Spirit of the Mountains" for the Four Seasons Hotel Whistler. Some of my favorite adaptations from that program appear in this book.

Method

To a Collins glass filled with cubed ice, add the whisky, maple syrup, vinegar, bitters, sparkling water, and cider. Stir gently to combine. For the garnish, use a peeler to remove a nice piece of peel from a washed lemon. Using a paring knife, trim the edges on all sides. Twist the peel to express the oil over the cocktail, then drop it into the glass.

Serves 1

Area of inspiration: Dehcho Region, Northwest Territories, Canada
Inspired by: the Shandy Gaff

———

¾ ounce (22.5 mL) Canadian 100% rye whisky

¾ ounce (22.5 mL) maple syrup

½ ounce (15 mL) apple cider vinegar

2 dashes grapefruit bitters
(like Bittered Sling Grapefruit & Hops)

3 ounces (90 mL) sparkling water

3 ounces (90 mL) sparkling apple cider
(alcoholic or nonalcoholic)

Garnish: Lemon twist

Betacillin

I've been lucky enough to travel to various parts of Ireland, and some of my memories are intertwined with chance encounters and spur-of-the-moment meetings. On one such occasion in Dublin, I ran into Tim Herlihy and Trevor Schneider, two great bartenders. At the time, Tim was the ambassador for an Irish whiskey brand, now the owner of the Lost Irish Whiskey brand, and he was so gracious, arranging a trip to the countryside so that Trevor (another ambassador from the United States) and I could visit a brand-new distillery under construction. This was really special. Between 1890 and 1966, all but two of the twenty-eight Irish distilleries had closed. In the 1980s, a third opened. As time carried on, the Irish whiskey category came back to life, and as of 2019, Ireland reported thirty-two working distilleries. Standing in the new distillery, I noticed that the giant copper pot stills had been placed and windows added, but there was still a lot of work to be done. Bartenders don't just create drinks and experiences; they live and breathe as part of our industry's culture, weathering storms, powering through challenging times, and sharing experiences with others, and the bar is always open. The Betacillin takes a modern classic—the Penicillin by Sam Ross—and twists it up for a unique experience inspired by the Irish countryside.

Method

To a shaker filled with cubed ice, add the whiskey, liqueur, carrot juice, lemon juice, syrup, and bitters. Using some force, shake hard for 10 seconds. Using a small, fine-mesh bar sieve to catch the loose ice chips, strain into a rocks glass filled with cubed ice. Garnish with the carrot slice. (Bonus points if the greens are still attached!)

Serves 1

Area of inspiration: County Offaly, Ireland
Inspired by: the Penicillin

———

1½ ounces (45 mL) Irish whiskey

½ ounce (15 mL) ginger liqueur

¾ ounce (22.5 mL) fresh carrot juice

¾ ounce (22.5 mL) fresh lemon juice

¾ ounce (22.5 mL) Honey Syrup (page 184)

2 dashes cherry bitters
(like Bittered Sling Suius Cherry)

Garnish: Small organic carrot slice (cut lengthwise), with greens

Stout, Stout, Let It All Out

This cocktail is inspired by new friendships worldwide and the certainty that there's an Irish pub with warm hospitality and service no matter where you are. Even when traveling alone, you never feel alone when you're in a pub, and it's always a wonderful place to kick back with old friends or make new ones. The original idea for this drink was a boilermaker, which is the blending of whisky and beer together, though they're rarely served in the same glass. Here, it becomes a beer cocktail of sorts. Now, you're either a lover or hater of stout. My first interaction with stout took place with my mom, brothers, and grandparents in a pub where we'd typically celebrate a special dinner, when we were too tired of the extravagant Sunday roasts. My grandfather Bryan waxed poetically with his cold stout in hand that stout was a great source of iron if you were deficient. At first, I cringed at the sip—after all, I was snatching small portions of spiced rum and tequila from the cabinet when no one was looking; I didn't have a taste for stout. But faced with the choice of that ice-cold, frothy stout, or the nearly room temperature Bass Ale or Boddington's, I opted to give it a shot. Today, all three pours are some of my favorites. Over the decades, many a pint and shot of whisky have been shared with friends from all over the world. I crave the thick, frothy top and the sensation as it melts away, cool and refreshing, while the dram (chosen by flavor or mood) adds that extra bit and continuation on the side. This cocktail is a lovely way to enjoy the flavors of stout and whisky together—a perfect pint, only made better with a side of fish and chips with mushy peas.

Method

To a Collins glass filled with cubed ice, add the whiskey, coffee, molasses, and bitters. Stir gently with a bar spoon to chill. Add more ice if necessary; it should be right to the top. Fill the glass with stout and tonic water, stirring just to combine.

Serves 1

Area of inspiration: Cape Town, South Africa
Inspired by: the Black and Tan

———

1 ounce (30 mL) Irish whiskey

2 ounces (60 mL) cold brewed coffee

½ ounce (15 mL) blackstrap molasses

2 dashes aromatic bitters
(like Bittered Sling Kensington)

2 ounces (60 mL) chilled stout (Guinness or Beamish)

2 ounces (60 mL) chilled tonic water

A PINT AMONG FRIENDS

It was 5:00 p.m. in Cape Town, and the competitors from a huge global bartending competition piled onto the stage in the main room of the Watershed. With the ocean crashing against the rocks in the background and the end-of-summer sun beaming through the windows, fifty-four bartenders stood shoulder to shoulder, stressed and looking around the room. Who would be the top six bartenders to carry on to the final challenge, the Cape Town Shakedown? The finalists would have twenty-four hours to build a bar program from scratch, from theme to décor to presentation to drinks, and showcase it to the 500-plus people in attendance.

I looked out to the crowd; there stood my coach and good friend, Grant Sceney, with a massive smile on his face. I remember thinking to myself, "We are going to make it, we will. The performances and drinks were amazing. Except for the speed round. Crap, I forgot about the speed round, that new shaker set split and killed the timing. Maybe those extra ten seconds overtime for all ten drinks won't matter. Or maybe they do matter." The inner monologue was killing me. I was shaking with nervous butterflies. Spike Merchant took the mic and started to build the crowd's excitement, and then silence. You could hear a pin drop. Names were called out, and mine wasn't one of them. The moment was over; I had lost. I was upset for two minutes, thinking in hindsight of my missteps and regrets, but overall I was happy with my performance. I was still the Canadian champ, full stop. The next day, after the Cape Town Shakedown, all the bartenders looked as stressed as they did excited. I found my fellow female competitors, Jasmin Rutter, Tess Posthumus, and Anna

Walsh to just stand still in the moment and digest what had happened. Naturally, we were so disappointed that no women were in the top six finale. Anna invited me out with the rest of her team for a pint of Guinness. As we walked together to an Irish pub, I realized that "a pint of Guinness" is a familiar ritual in most countries, and there's more to my life than winning and losing—it's about friendships. From that moment, Anna and I built a friendship that's been going strong for years. Usually, Anna is the first person I call when I land in Ireland and the last person I see before I depart—all with a pint of Guinness. Both Anna and I felt the same about this global competition. The advice we gave each other in the moment is still the advice we give to the younger generations as they prepare for their global battles: use the opportunity to show what you can do and remember, this could be an audition for something bigger; you never know who's watching. Anna is focused on developing alcohol-free beverage programs but always leaves room for a Guinness with friends.

Glacial Snout

Part of the reason I love cocktails is their ability to connect us to the land. Scotch whiskies are unique for many reasons, and the terroir from region to region, along with the distillery style, creates an infinite number of tastes to discover. Scotland itself is stunning and picturesque. The brisk waters of the Atlantic rush against the shores in the west, smashing the jagged cliffs in all directions with salt and brine, and affecting the spirits and vegetation. To the east, lowlands and rolling hills stretch all the way to the coast, with spongy peat bogs and wild heather as far as the eye can see. A bird's eye view of Scotland shows the thousands of tiny lakes formed by the last Ice Age, 2.6 million years ago. Located in what was called the "snout of the glacier," an inspiring name for a cocktail if I've ever heard one, the Isle of Skye in particular is special. Its mountains and coloration are vastly different than I've seen elsewhere, like they were pulled from a fantasy movie. It's a memorable place that feels so remote, nestled among challenging terrain and sea. The ideal way to recreate and cherish the moment is to have a drink in hand with great people at a local oyster or lobster stand with a postcard view. I was thrilled to feature this on the Four Seasons Hotel Vancouver Ocean's Program.

Method

To a shaker filled with cubed ice, add the whisky, Chartreuse, lemon juice, syrup, and bitters. Using some force, shake hard for 5 seconds. Using a small fine-mesh bar sieve to catch the loose ice chips, double strain into a cocktail glass or coupe. Garnish with a rosemary sprig on a clip.

Serves 1

Area of inspiration: Isle of Skye, Scotland
Inspired by: the Champs-Élysées

———

1½ ounces (45 mL) Isle of Skye whisky
(like Talisker)

½ ounce (15 mL) yellow Chartreuse

½ ounce (15 mL) fresh lemon juice

¼ ounce (7.5 mL) Rosemary Syrup (page 185)

2 dashes celery bitters
(like Bittered Sling Cascade Celery)

Garnish: Fresh rosemary sprig

Loup-Garou

In 2015, I had an idea to blend my love of supernatural horror stories and cocktails. Inspired by the 1961 film *La Nuit du Loup-Garou* and "The Wolf Theme" from Sergei Prokofiev's symphony *Peter and the Wolf*, I got to work. I was working on a presentation for a competition, and I thought if I could use music and sound to affect the environment, remove the judges' sight long enough to encourage visualization, and bring in other sensory elements, I'd have an excellent shot at winning the challenge. I contacted Johnathon Vaughn Strebly, a friend from Vancouver, and told him I needed a French hornist trio to perform a minute-and-a-half classical composition in Chicago. Johnathon was friends with the president of the Vancouver Symphony Orchestra, who connected us to the director of orchestra personnel for the Chicago Symphony Orchestra, who introduced us to three talented French hornists. When the day came, I was so excited. The drink was delicious, and the pieces had all come together. The judges came in, and I realized I was competing at the same time as three other bartenders, and we only had pipe and drape separating us—no walls. I asked the judges to blindfold themselves, lit a piece of peat bog on fire, and in the voice of an eerie 1960s broadcast narrator, recited a soliloquy about Scotland's moors and what waits for you in the darkness: the werewolves. I then asked the judges to open their eyes. The table was dressed in a player piano song scroll edge to edge, with cut-out black-and-white comics arranged to tell a scary story about monsters in the darkness. On the table was a 1979 Universal Movie Monsters lunchbox, filled with mushrooms and soil, with a plastic hand emerging and holding a decanter filled with the perfectly stirred, chilled, and diluted cocktail. The judges, Julie Reiner and Charles Joly, were asked to pick up the decanter and pour the drink into small clay cups with frozen silver bullet whisky stones to keep the cups cold and protect them, as only a silver bullet can, from what came next. Just then, the three musicians—Matthew Oliphant, Allison Tutton, and Alex Laskey—walked in and "The Wolf Theme" rang out. The judges were speechless, and so was I. Time was up. And I won.

Serves 2

Area of inspiration: Chicago, Illinois
Inspired by: the Vieux Carré

———

3 ounces (90 mL) blended scotch whisky

1 ounce (30 mL) Islay whisky

1½ ounces (45 mL) Infrared Red Vermouth (page 238) or red vermouth

½ ounce (15 mL) Boréal Cordial (page 66)

2 dashes spicy aromatic bitters
(like Bittered Sling Moondog Latin)

2 dashes celery bitters
(like Bittered Sling Cascade Celery)

Garnish: Local heather and grasses, tied around the decanter

Method

Fill a mixing glass with cubed ice. Add the whiskies, vermouth, cordial, and both bitters. Stir with a bar spoon for 15 to 20 rotations. Using a julep strainer, strain into a chilled decanter. Place on ice and serve in small tasting glasses or clay cups.

Mise en Place Recipes

Balsam Fir Spray

Makes 3¼ ounces (95 mL)

2 ounces (60 mL) filtered water

1¼ ounces (35 mL) vodka

2 drops balsam fir essential oil (see note)

In a small atomizer, combine the water, vodka, and essential oil. Close the lid and shake. Store in the fridge for up to 6 months.

Note: Use only natural, pure balsam fir essential oil (no carrier oils) and use a pipette to add just 2 drops. The oil is highly concentrated, and 2 drops are enough to aromatize. Store essential oils in the fridge in sealed containers.

———

Cherry Cola Cordial

Makes 16 ounces (500 mL)

1 kilogram cherries, pitted

1-inch (2.5 cm) piece fresh ginger

300 grams superfine or granulated sugar

15 grams citric acid

15 grams gum arabic powder

⅓ ounce (10 mL) Cola Flower Water (page 185)

Set up a juicer. Juice the cherries, then strain. Juice the ginger into a separate container, then strain. You should have about 10 ounces (300 mL) cherry juice and 1 ounce (30 mL) ginger juice. Add the juices to a blender, along with the sugar, citric acid, gum arabic, and Cola Flower Water. Blend on medium until the sugar is dissolved. Strain the liquid through cheesecloth to microfilter. This syrup should be vibrant and red. Store in a sanitized bottle, labeled with the date, in the fridge for up to 10 days.

Cola Flower Water

Makes 3½ ounces (100 mL)

2 ounces (60 mL) filtered water

1¼ ounces (35 mL) white rum

2 drops nutmeg essential oil

2 drops cinnamon essential oil

3 drops lemon essential oil

2 drops orange essential oil

1 drop lavender essential oil

3 drops vanilla essential oil

In a small jar or bottle, combine the water, rum, and essential oils. Close the lid and shake. Refrigerate for 4 days, shaking a couple of times a day. Strain through a paper coffee filter to microfilter. Pour into a bottle with a pipette dropper, label with the date, and store in the fridge for up to 6 months.

Note: Use only natural, pure essential oils (no carrier oils) and use a pipette to add only the amounts listed in the recipe. These oils are highly concentrated. Store essential oils in the fridge in sealed containers.

Honey Syrup

Makes 10 ounces (300 mL)

200 grams raw honey

7 ounces (200 mL) filtered water

In a nonreactive container, whisk the honey and water until combined. (Do not heat.) Store in a sanitized bottle, labeled with the date, in the fridge for up to 10 days.

Note: Flavors and styles of honey vary, so this is a great opportunity to experiment with honeys from your local purveyors.

Jaffa Orange Crush Cordial

Makes 16 ounces (500 mL)

300 grams superfine or granulated sugar

100 grams fresh orange peels (from 5 oranges)

5 grams dried edible roses

15 grams gum arabic powder

15 grams citric acid

5 ounces (150 mL) freshly squeezed orange juice

4 ounces (125 mL) water

1 ounce (30 mL) fresh ginger juice

2 drops rose water

Add the sugar, orange peels, and roses to an airtight container and press with a muddler. Let stand for 24 hours. The next day, transfer the mixture to a blender and add the gum arabic, citric acid, orange juice, water, ginger juice, and rose water. Blend on medium until the sugar is dissolved. Strain the liquid through a mesh sieve, then through cheesecloth to microfilter. Store in a sanitized bottle, labeled with the date, in the fridge for up to 10 days.

Rosemary Syrup

Makes 10 ounces (300 mL)

1 branch fresh rosemary (10 grams)

200 grams sugar

7 ounces (200 mL) filtered water

Cut the rosemary into manageable sprigs with leaves. In a small saucepan over low heat, combine the sugar and water, stirring until the sugar is dissolved. Add the rosemary. Bring to a boil, then turn off the heat, cover, and steep until cool. Strain the liquid through a mesh sieve, then through cheesecloth to microfilter. Store in a sanitized bottle, labeled with the date, in the fridge for up to 10 days.

Wine

Bajan Apéritif

Jackie Summers is a newish friend of mine. He's of Bajan descent and lives in Brooklyn, and is a brilliant writer, activist, liqueur maker, and businessperson. We've spent a few years on an educational committee together, and whether we're discussing our favorite vegetables or hot sauce recipes or the importance of standing up for what you believe in, I always leave our conversations feeling inspired. And as an activist and communicator, Jackie has helped me better understand his world and the challenges he faces as a person of color within our industry. Jackie is also the developer behind Sorel Liqueur, a product designed to bring a piece of Barbados and his heritage to the bottle. Based on a 500-year-old beverage, the liqueur is full of hibiscus and warm spices, and this cocktail draws on Jackie's favorite flavors.

Method

Add cubed ice to a Lewis bag and smash into chips with a mallet. Fill a Collins glass halfway with crushed ice and add the wine, agua fresca, vermouth, syrup, and bitters. Stir gently with a bar spoon to chill. Add more crushed ice to fill right to the top. Garnish with the rosemary and thyme. Serve with a long, wide reusable or compostable straw.

Serves 1

Area of inspiration: Brooklyn, New York, by way of Barbados
Inspired by: the Bamboo

———

1½ ounces (45 mL) rosé wine

1 ounce (30 mL) Hibiscus Agua Fresca (page 132)

1 ounce (30 mL) rosé vermouth

½ ounce (15 mL) Bajan Spice Syrup (page 212)

2 dashes orange bitters
(like Bittered Sling Orange & Juniper)

Garnish: Fresh rosemary sprig, fresh thyme sprig

Bottleshock

The Judgement of Paris wine tasting competition of 1976 saw the 1973 vintage of Chateau Montelena's Chardonnay receiving top honors in a blind tasting, alongside another noteworthy burgundy. This was not just a testament to California's wine country, but a celebration of the constant innovation being demonstrated throughout the state by winemakers and viticulturists alike, bringing the very best vintages to the 3,500 restaurants in San Francisco. While I would never recommend blending something as unique as Chateau Montelena with anything but tears of joy, this cocktail is a recognition of the delicious power of Napa Valley's wine region. It shows us there's something for everyone, from the top-tier wine enthusiast, collector, and sommelier to the day-to-day lover of wine discoveries and experiences. As a sommelier, I'm always studying wine regions and grape varietals and adding their tasting notes to my brain's aroma Rolodex. I hope this spin on the white wine spritzer captures everyone and changes the meaning of ABC from "Anything but Chardonnay" to "Another Beautiful Chardonnay." I featured this drink on the Four Seasons San Francisco's "Fog City Tales" menu in 2019.

Method

Add cubed ice to a Lewis bag and smash into chips with a mallet. Fill a large wineglass halfway with crushed ice and add the Chardonnay, liqueur, cordial, and bitters. Stir with a swizzle stick or bar spoon to agitate, chill, and dilute. Add the coconut water, stir, and top with more crushed ice. Garnish with the coconut curls, cantaloupe, and mint. Serve with a long, wide reusable or compostable straw.

Serves 1

Area of inspiration: Napa Valley, California
Inspired by: White Sangria

———

2 ounces (60 mL) Cantaloupe Chardonnay (page 213)

½ ounce (15 mL) coconut liqueur

¾ ounce (22.5 mL) Turmeric & Ginger Cordial (page 215)

2 dashes lemon bitters
(like Bittered Sling Lem-Marrakech)

2 ounces (60 mL) chilled sparkling coconut water (like La Croix)

Garnish: Toasted coconut curls, thin cantaloupe slice (skin on), fresh mint

Champagne Josephine

In 2004, I walked into my interview at Le Sélect Bistro. I had long dark-red hair and a long purple knitted jacket, and my "punk rock meets sixties pin-up" look was tailored for Toronto's Queen West (if you know, you know). The iconic restaurant had been around since 1977, owned by "the cook," Frédéric Giesweiller (from Alsace), "the nose," Jean-Jacques Quinsac (from Provence), and Vicki Quinsac (JJ's wife, from Cincinnati, the legendary and super-chic restaurant manager). I was applying as a bartender for the summer. The restaurant had just moved to its new home on Wellington Street in the Garment District. Jean-Jacques was interviewing me. "Lauren, I'm not sure if you will fit in here. Do you know wine? Do you know French food?" His questions were valid. This wasn't a summer-bistro whatever job; this was about bringing the best of France to Toronto. "Jean-Jacques, I am hardworking, energetic, speak French, and am studying French cuisine, culture, and wine. I will work harder for you than anyone. Please, take a chance on me." I stayed with the company for four years and made some of the most incredible friendships of my life under that roof. Over the years, I moved into different positions to learn as much as possible, and served celebrities and diplomats alike at the bar as weekly regulars, including the legendary musician Daniel Lanois. I read the massive wine book JJ created, which I still hold dear in my Amsterdam book collection, and learned about Frédéric's obsession with light dimmers and musical choices and volume. But the biggest lesson was the importance of working face to face—owners to the team, owners to guests, owners to family. We're not sure who came up with the cocktails on the back of the giant menu at Le Sélect Bistro, but they were not often ordered. One night, an order came in for a champagne Josephine. My work friend Martin McNenly and I had no idea what it was, but we laughed and did the best we could, following the flavors in the description. This rendition will do us all justice and uphold the Le Sélect Bistro culture, especially as JJ and Frédéric have now passed the torch of their business to new owners. What a legacy to leave behind.

Serves 1

Area of inspiration: Toronto, Ontario
Inspired by: the French 75

¾ ounce (22.5 mL) gin

½ ounce (15 mL) framboise eau de vie

¾ ounce (22.5 mL) Lavender Cordial (page 214)

2 dashes celery bitters
(like Bittered Sling Cascade Celery)

Ice-cold champagne

Garnish: Lemon twist

Method

To a shaker filled with cubed ice, add the gin, framboise, cordial, and bitters. Using some force, shake hard for 5 seconds. Using a small fine-mesh bar sieve to catch the loose ice chips, double strain into a champagne flute or white wineglass. Check the champagne to make sure it's not flat, then slowly top the cocktail with the cold, fresh champagne. For the garnish, use a peeler to remove a nice piece of peel from a washed lemon. Using a paring knife, trim the edges on all sides. Twist the peel to express the oil over the cocktail, then drop it into the glass.

It's Jammy

In 2013, I attended a luncheon in New Orleans with the Ladies United for the Preservation of Endangered Cocktails. The LUPEC community celebrates women in the bartending profession while raising funds for women's charities. Lynnette Marrero, who invited me, was the president of the New York chapter. Mutual friends in the industry had connected us, and this first meeting opened up conversations I was anxious to have, as I wanted to bring something like LUPEC to Canada. I was walking into a world I hadn't known existed: a good group of women in the drinks industry, so colorful in their dress and personalities, getting together to talk advancement, development, and respect. I knew Lynnette as the cofounder of Speed Rack with Ivy Mix, and was anxious to chat about what we could do in Canada together. I sat down at the table and chatted with women I had hero-worshipped from afar. It was one of the most important moments of my professional and personal life. Following this gathering, Lynnette became a mentor from afar, and we worked on several initiatives together, first through Speed Rack and eventually through other programs worldwide. After almost a decade, we are closer than ever, with mutual respect and love. We have the same focus: amplifying the voices of women and other groups that are underrepresented in the drinks industry. It's Jammy is a great way to commemorate our ongoing friendship. A big thank you to Lynnette for writing the foreword to this book too!

Serves 4

Area of inspiration: New Orleans, Louisiana
Inspired by: the Delmonico

———

10 ounces (300 mL) Rioja red wine

2 ounces (60 mL) Spanish brandy

1 ounce (30 mL) verjuice (red or white)

1 ounce (30 mL) Blood Orange Grenadine
(page 213)

12 ounces (375 mL) Strawberry Beer (page 215)

4 dashes cherry bitters
(like Bittered Sling Suius Cherry)

Garnish: 4 dehydrated or fresh blood orange wheels

Method
Fill a 1-quart (1 L) water pitcher with ice. Add the wine, brandy, verjuice, grenadine, Strawberry Beer, and bitters. Stir gently with a bar spoon to chill. Using a julep strainer, strain into a decanter and add a sidecar of ice and tongs. As the pitcher is quite big, take your time to strain this, using two hands to keep the pitcher and strainer secure. For each portion, pour 6½ ounces (190 mL) into each of four wineglasses. Add a side serve of blood orange wheels so that guests can add both garnish and ice as they like.

Cold as Rice

Masa Shiroki is the owner and winemaker of Vancouver's Artisan Sake Maker. Born in Fukui, Japan, 60 miles (100 km) north of Kyoto, Masa is a mastermind. His lineup of sakes differs from bottle to bottle, and he has worked tirelessly to develop a product rooted in the Japanese style but brought to life in Canada. Throughout the years, Masa has supported the bartending community in Vancouver, from sponsored events and tastings to training and cocktail development, and he sees the opportunity for creativity when it comes to enjoying sake on its own or in mixed drinks. In 2015, Masa announced that he had selected a northern Japanese seed of rice from the Nanatsuboshi varietal and was producing the first-ever 100 percent Canadian-made sake. Masa's rice paddy in Fraser Valley, British Columbia, has the ideal conditions, with glacial waters, great soil, and lots of sunshine, giving the rice its rich flavor. When Jonathan and I opened Kale & Nori in 2011, Masa gave us $500 as a "help you get started" gift. He's a total legend. This drink is a creamy spin on a Daisy cocktail with nigori sake, and is a brand-new take on beautiful, handmade rice wine, something I imagine would make Masa smile. Make sure you taste the sake on its own first to appreciate the mastery—the tropical notes, aroma, and texture.

Method

To a shaker filled with cubed ice, add the sake, lychee puree, shrub, and soy sauce. Using some force, shake hard for 5 seconds. Using a small fine-mesh bar sieve to catch the loose ice chips, double strain into a highball glass.

Serves 1

Area of inspiration: Fraser Valley, British Columbia
Inspired by: the Daisy

———

2 ounces (60 mL) good-quality junmai nigori unfiltered sake

2 ounces (60 mL) lychee puree

1 ounce (30 mL) Ginger Shrub (page 93)

1 dash white soy sauce or Saline Solution (page 95)

Peaskeeper

Bartenders are the peacekeepers of bars and restaurants. They speak culinarily, create magic for guests, and innovate for the future. I remember one evening when I was working alongside a host of chefs at a culinary festival in London. Chefs Manu Buffara (Brazil), Niklas Ekstedt (Sweden), and Magnus Nilsson (Sweden) cooked for and entertained a full chef's table night after night while I created cocktails to pair with the food. It takes a lot of time and study to grow a relationship with chefs, to understand the technical aspects, gastronomic history, and flavor of their dishes. The chefs and I had a great time sharing our ideas. The Peaskeeper celebrates the special relationship we bartenders experience working in a hospitality team that protects and looks out for each other, though we all have different personalities, strengths, skills, and backgrounds. The "Peas" part of the name comes from the zero-proof spirit Seedlip Garden 108, made from snap peas, and "peacekeeper" tips the hat to the hospitality professionals who work each day to create safe and inclusive environments for people to experience something special. A big thank you to my friends Ben Branson and Claire Warner for all the love and passion you put into the Seedlip and Seedlip Aperitivo brands.

Method

To a shaker filled with cubed ice, add the sake, Seedlip Garden, cordial, and bitters. Using some force, shake hard for 5 seconds. Using a small fine-mesh bar sieve to catch the loose ice chips, strain over an ice sphere in a coupe glass. Garnish with the origami crane.

Serves 1

Area of inspiration: London, England
Inspired by: the Aviation

———

1 ounce (30 mL) Sake with Pineapple (page 214; see note)

1 ounce (30 mL) Seedlip Garden 108 nonalcoholic spirits

1 ounce (30 mL) Lavender Cordial (page 214)

2 dashes cherry bitters
(like Bittered Sling Suius Cherry)

Garnish: Origami crane

Note: To make this cocktail fully nonalcoholic, replace the sake in the Sake with Pineapple recipe with Seedlip Dry Aperitivo.

Déjà Brew

In 2012, Jonathan and I put together a contest of "who will propose first," thinking if we made a game out of it that it would seem less like marriage and more like an adventure. During a trip to the Okanagan Valley for work later that summer, our friends Cameron Smith and Dana Ewart, the owners of Joy Road Catering, invited us to their God's Mountain al fresco dinner with fifty other people, overlooking stunning Skaha Lake right at magic hour. Dana stood up and recited a passage from Alice Waters's cookbook to inspire everyone to think about the produce, the dishes, and the community dining together. The breeze was sweet and cool, aromatic with flowers and fresh herbs, with a gentle humidity that was comfortable for the glorious summer night. Course after course arrived, each as simple, delicious, and beautiful as the last. I left to wander the grounds and came back to a shaky Jonathan. I sat down and, all of a sudden, a platter of kale and nori arrived from the kitchen with my grandparents' engagement rings from the 1940s woven through lavender sprigs. This was it! Jonathan got down on his knee and proposed—the sheer shock of it all! Then I realized I would have to propose at some point, so I got down on my knee and did the same. It was an incredible evening spent with fifty new friends, Jonathan's romantic gesture complemented by the mastery of our good friends Cam and Dana. This simple dessert cocktail always reminds me of that most perfect moment in the beaming sunset of God's Mountain. Déjà Brew is a delicious riff on the affogato, a classic ice cream and espresso pairing, but this one is dressed differently with tea, a really good ice cream, a crunchy topping, and a digestif cocktail. If you've got access to some vintage cups and saucers, like the ones I have from my grandmother Florence, that makes this drink all the more special.

Serves 4

Area of inspiration: God's Mountain, British Columbia
Inspired by: the Affogato

———

2 ounces (60 mL) amontillado sherry

2 ounces (60 mL) bourbon

1¼ ounces (35 mL) amaretto liqueur

4 ounces (125 mL) chilled Cardamom Black Tea (page 213)

2 ounces (60 mL) maple syrup

8 dashes (8 mL) chocolate bitters (like Bittered Sling Malagasy Chocolate)

8 small scoops coconut ice cream

Garnish (optional): 40 grams toasted unsweetened coconut flakes, 40 grams chopped pine nuts

Method

To a mixing glass, add the sherry, bourbon, amaretto, tea, maple syrup, and bitters, stirring to combine. Keep chilled until ready to serve. When ready, lay out four teacups with saucers and demitasse spoons. Add 2 small scoops of ice cream to each cup. Serve tableside, pouring 2½ ounces (75 mL) of the tea mixture over the ice cream in each cup. For the garnish, combine the coconut and pine nuts on a dish and serve with a demitasse spoon, passing the crunchy topping around for guests to help themselves. Marriage proposal optional.

Iberian Apéritif

A few years ago, I was invited as a guest for a food and beverage symposium in Barcelona. I was honored to join such culinary and wine dignitaries as Josep Roca (one of the famed brothers behind El Celler de Can Roca) and François Chartier (the author of *Taste Buds and Molecules*). After the show, Jonathan and I moved from our glam hotel in the north of the city to an Airbnb in the Gothic Quarter. It was in an old five-story walk-up without electricity. To put this in context, we were on our three-week honeymoon, and Barcelona was our first stop. We also travel like North Americans: big suitcases, too many pairs of shoes and outfits, and not nearly enough room for the tinned fish we bought to bring back home. Nevertheless, once we hoofed everything up the narrow, rickety cement staircase, we realized it was worth every step. The sunbeams sending highlights over El Raval, and the classic cocktail journey we'd embark on later that night with friends, Andrea Montague and Stuart Hudson, would prove this, as well. If you're ever in the neighborhood, begin at Dry Martini, move on to Boadas, then Caribbean Club, and end up at the Absenta del Raval. These days, it's more exciting to split up a pub crawl over several nights while adding some great tapas and a visit to some of the new bars that illustrate how Barcelona makes cocktails today, like Paradiso, SIPS, and Two Schmucks. No matter how you spend your days or evenings, there's one thing we can all agree on: sherry is the queen of the Spanish drinking experience, as you'll pleasantly discover with this Iberian Apéritif.

Method

Fill a mixing glass with cubed ice. Add the sherries, brandy, curaçao, syrup, and bitters. Stir gently with a bar spoon to chill. Using a julep strainer, strain into a Nick and Nora glass or coupette. Serve with a ramekin of Smoked Olives, a pit tray, and a pick.

Serves 1

Area of inspiration: Barcelona, Spain
Inspired by: the Adonis

———

1 ounce (30 mL) dry amontillado sherry

1 ounce (30 mL) PX sherry

1 ounce (30 mL) Spanish brandy

¼ ounce (7.5 mL) Saffron Curaçao (page 214)

¼ ounce (7.5 mL) coconut flower syrup (available online)

2 dashes lemon bitters
(like Bittered Sling Lem-Marrakech)

Side: Smoked Olives (recipe follows)

Smoked Olives

Fill a handheld smoker chamber with applewood chips and ensure it is connected securely to the smoking box via the hose connector. Place 500 grams green Castelvetrano olives in a shallow container or bowl in the smoking box and close and latch the door. Turn on the handheld smoker and let the chamber fill with smoke for 10 seconds. Turn off the smoker and let stand for 10 to 15 seconds. Repeat five times. Let the olives stand in the chamber for 15 minutes before removing. Use immediately or store in an airtight container, labeled with the date, in the fridge for up to 5 days.

Open Sesame

I'd never been particularly fond of halva, the sweet sesame and honey dessert from the Middle East. But my time in Israel changed how I think about it. When I landed in Israel for the first time, the first place I wanted to visit with Oron Lerner, a well-known Israeli bartender, was a market. The display of challah, spices, halva, and local produce was incredible; it gave me such an appreciation for the foods I only had access to at my grandmother's house or certain friends' and family's homes. I returned to Israel with a chef friend a few years later, and we immediately headed to another market. We spent hours ducking in and out of shops and cafés, tasting this and that, and just being in the moment with the flavors and aromas. The mountains of rugelach, overflowing towers of sesame seeds and za'atar, perfect falafels, street foods, and, yes, halva were inspiring. This drink is the ultimate celebration of my discovery of the flavors of my heritage, and my ode to sesame and other flavors in Jewish cuisine that work so well together.

Method

To a shaker, add the port, scotch, orgeat, bitters, and the whole egg. Dry shake (without ice) for 5 seconds to emulsify the ingredients. Open the shaker and add cubed ice. Using some force, shake hard for 10 seconds. Using a small fine-mesh bar sieve to catch the loose ice chips, double strain into a port or dessert wineglass. Garnish with cinnamon and sesame seeds. Serve with a slice of babka or a cinnamon bun on the side.

Serves 1

Area of inspiration: Tel Aviv, Israel
Inspired by: the Coffee Cocktail

——

1½ ounces (45 mL) tawny port

1½ ounces (45 mL) blended scotch whisky

¾ ounce (22.5 mL) Babka Orgeat (page 212)

2 dashes coffee bitters
(like Bittered Sling Arabica Coffee)

1 egg (see note)

Garnish and Side: Grated cinnamon, sesame seeds, slice of babka (cinnamon and raisin preferred!) or cinnamon bun

Note: If you are concerned about the food safety of raw eggs, use 2 ounces (60 mL) pasteurized liquid whole eggs in place of the egg.

Quite Apeeling

If we are able to take a road trip rather than a plane trip, we always do. It's nice to move at your own pace, stop in different towns, and sightsee. On the coast of Portugal, the terrain changes so rapidly, as does the altitude and the ocean's temperature and power. The cliffs hang over the Atlantic, the breeze is salty, and in the hottest weather, that smack of chilled air is just the best. Madeira, the fortified wine similar to sherry that is produced on the Portuguese island of the same name, is often overlooked. The flavors seem light and fluffy at times, and at others, creamy, tropical, and salty. Walking along the cliffs, I looked out over the horizon toward Madeira and wondered why more people don't talk about this fantastic wine. It's certainly something to enjoy and appreciate while you're in the country. If you're lucky enough to have access to this wine where you are, try it a few different ways. I lean toward tropical recipes in the summer months, inspired by summer travels. After I did some experiments with tepache-style fermented beverages from other fruits, banana tepache quickly became a staple. The flavor combination of banana, strawberry, and Madeira is extraordinary and makes a great template for other tropical, easy-drinking, complex summer beverages.

Method

To a highball glass filled with cubed ice, add the Madeira, tepache, shrub, and bitters. Stir gently with a bar spoon to chill. Add more ice if necessary; it should be right to the top. For the garnish, use a peeler to remove a long piece of peel from a washed orange. Using a paring knife, trim the edges on all sides. Twist the peel to express the oil over the cocktail, then drop it into the glass.

Serves 1

Area of inspiration: coastal Portugal
Inspired by: the Sherry Highball

———

2 ounces (60 mL) Madeira

3 ounces (90 mL) Banana Tepache (page 213)

1½ ounces (45 mL) Strawberry Shrub (page 215)

3 dashes peach bitters
(like Bittered Sling Clingstone Peach)

Garnish: Long orange twist

Black Forest

Having lived close to the British Columbia wine-making region for years (and having a mild obsession with wine), I can confidently say you'll have a fantastic experience if you can get to a wine-making area during crush season—the time of year when the grapes are perfectly ripe across vineyards. In September/October in the northern hemisphere or February/March in the southern hemisphere, vineyards are in full swing. Sebastian Brack and Maximillian Wagner, the founders of Belsazar, a vermouth company in the south of Germany, invited me to visit the three critical areas of their operation after completing a program I was running in Berlin. The weather was still great, and the crush was underway. The first stop was the vineyard, walking between the rows with the third-generation winemaker from Zähringer vineyards, a glass of their wine in hand. The next stop was the winery itself, where white and black grapes are sorted, stemmed, pressed, and fermented with some overly talkative wine barrels chirping in the cellar as the wines mature. These wines are carefully selected as the base for the vermouths, and they'll be aromatized with herbs and botanicals, ready for the next stage. Our final stop, the Schladerer distillery, about a thirty-minute drive away, took us deeper into the Black Forest. This distillery, family owned since 1844, distills various fruits into brilliant eaux de vies, which then act as the fortifying liquids that bring the texture and ABV level up on the vermouths while lending some distinct flavors to the final product. After leaving the distillery, we couldn't resist the temptation of stopping at a café in the middle of the green fields, rolling hills, and thick brush of trees to have a slice of Black Forest cake in the Black Forest. This drink encapsulates those flavors.

Serves 1

Area of inspiration: Black Forest, Germany
Inspired by: the Port Wine Cocktail

———

1 ounce (30 mL) rosé vermouth

1 ounce (30 mL) Pineau des Charentes fortified wine

½ ounce (15 mL) kirsch eau de vie

½ ounce (15 mL) Raspberry & Coconut Shrub (page 214)

2 dashes chocolate bitters
(like Bittered Sling Malagasy Chocolate)

Garnish: Lemon twist

Method

Fill a mixing glass with cubed ice. Add the vermouth, Pineau, kirsch, shrub, and bitters. Stir gently with a bar spoon to chill. Using a julep strainer, strain into a chilled dessert wineglass. For the garnish, use a peeler to remove a nice piece of peel from a washed lemon. Cut the sides into a diamond shape. Add a lengthwise slit to the center of the peel, without cutting through to the edges, and rest it on the rim of the glass.

24 Hours of Darkness

Back in the winter of 2015, I visited Reykjavik, Iceland, for the first time with friends Shawn Soole, Chris Purcell, and Tyler Mackenzie. The sun didn't come up at all—there was twenty-four hours of darkness. I had been expecting the drinks to be as explosive as the geography, but as it turned out, the philosophy was quite simple: use in-season flavors, celebrate local (a lot of local beers), and enjoy with friends. Apart from the beer fermented with sheep poop and an obsession with white Russians and fermented shark, I chased aquavit, a dry spirit from Scandinavia with different styles across the Nordics and Iceland. It's flavored with caraway and sometimes dill and coriander. I used aquavit the same way I would gin; it provides a different flavor, but complements the taste of Icelandic regional ingredients perfectly. What grows together usually goes together. I have fond memories of spending time with amazing people in Iceland, enjoying late-night hot dogs with special Icelandic mustard, discovering one of my favorite bands—GusGus—during the Airwaves Music Festival, and traveling to the Blue Lagoon hot springs. This cocktail is crisp, savory, and palate cleansing, and has nothing in common with a white Russian, thank goodness.

Method

To a shaker filled with cubed ice, add the vermouth, aquavit, apéritif, grapefruit juice, lemon juice, and bitters. Using some force, shake hard for 5 seconds. Using a small fine-mesh bar sieve to catch the loose ice chips, double strain into a rocks glass filled with cubed ice. For the garnish, use a peeler to remove a nice piece of peel from a washed grapefruit. Cut the sides into a diamond shape. Add a lengthwise slit to the center of the peel, without cutting through to the edges, and rest it on the rim of the glass.

Serves 1

Area of inspiration: Reykjavik, Iceland
Inspired by: the Paper Plane

———

¾ ounce (22.5 mL) Starlight White Vermouth (page 239) or white vermouth

¾ ounce (22.5 mL) Icelandic aquavit (like Brennivín)

¾ ounce (22.5 mL) rhubarb apéritif (like Aperol)

¾ ounce (22.5 mL) fresh grapefruit juice

¼ ounce (7.5 mL) fresh lemon juice

2 dashes grapefruit bitters (like Bittered Sling Grapefruit & Hops)

Garnish: Grapefruit twist

Mise en Place Recipes

Babka Orgeat

Makes 16 ounces (500 mL)

1 cinnamon stick

300 grams white sesame seeds

60 grams golden raisins

10 ounces (300 mL) filtered water

300 grams superfine or granulated sugar

Pinch kosher salt

½ ounce (15 mL) white rum

1 drop orange flower water

In a nonreactive container, combine the cinnamon stick, sesame seeds, raisins, and water. Cover and refrigerate for 24 hours. The next day, transfer the mixture (including the cinnamon and raisins) to a blender, along with the sugar, salt, rum, and flower water. Blend on medium until the sugar is dissolved. Strain the liquid through cheesecloth and wring out the cheesecloth. (Reserve the seed mixture for another use if you wish.) Store in a sanitized bottle, labeled with the date, in the fridge for up to 10 days.

Bajan Spice Syrup

Makes 10 ounces (300 mL)

200 grams Demerara sugar

7 ounces (200 mL) filtered water

4 whole cloves

½ Scotch bonnet chili pepper (see note)

6 grams lime peels

4 grams allspice berries

4 grams whole black peppercorns

4 grams fresh rosemary, roughly chopped

4 grams fresh thyme, roughly chopped

2 grams cumin seeds

2 grams smashed nutmeg pieces

2 grams cinnamon stick

Pinch salt

Using an immersion circulator, bring a pot of water to 195°F (90°C) (or use a stem thermometer to hold the temperature on medium-high heat). In a bowl, whisk together the sugar and water until the sugar is dissolved. Add the remaining ingredients to a heatproof food-safe bag and top with the sugar water. Remove the air from the bag, seal, and clip it to the side of the pot, ensuring that the mixture is underwater. Cook for 1½ hours. Transfer the bag to an ice bath and let cool. Strain the liquid into a sanitized bottle, label with the date, and store in the fridge for up to 10 days.

Note: If you prefer slightly less heat, remove the seeds from the chili pepper before adding it to the bag.

Banana Tepache

Makes 1½ quarts (1.5 L)

110 grams Demerara or dark brown sugar

1½ quarts (1.5 L) cold filtered water

2 whole ripe bananas (with peels), washed and cut into ½-inch (1 cm) slices

2 ounces (60 mL) Pineapple Tepache (page 113) or any other ferment starter

In a large bowl, whisk together the sugar and water until the sugar is dissolved. Add the banana slices to a 2-quart (2 L) jar, preferably with an air lock (see note). Top with the sugar water and Pineapple Tepache (the live, active ferment; a SCOBY is not necessary here). Fold a paper coffee filter in half and place on top of the banana slices, pressing to soak, to keep the fruit submerged and moist. Close the lid. After 5 days, strain the liquid and filter using a large mesh strainer into smaller bottles with rubber flip tops. Label with the date and store in the fridge for up to 6 months, burping every few days. Reserve some of the SCOBY for a future Banana Tepache starter.

Note: If you don't have a jar with an air lock, just close the lid and remember to "burp" the jar each day to release the carbon dioxide, a by-product of fermentation.

Blood Orange Grenadine

Makes 8 ounces (250 mL)

4 blood oranges

150 grams superfine or granulated sugar

4 grams citric acid

2 drops orange flower water

2 drops rose water

Juice the blood oranges. Strain the juice to remove the pulp and measure 5 ounces (150 mL). Add the juice, sugar, citric acid, and flower waters to a blender. Blend on medium until the sugar is dissolved. Strain the liquid through cheesecloth to microfilter. Store in a sanitized bottle, labeled with the date, in the fridge for up to 10 days.

Cantaloupe Chardonnay

Makes 16 ounces (500 mL), 10% ABV

190 grams chopped peeled cantaloupe

2 cups (500 mL) high-quality Chardonnay wine

Add the cantaloupe and Chardonnay to a 1-quart (1 L) jar. Fold a paper coffee filter in half and place on top of the cantaloupe, pressing to soak, to keep the fruit submerged and moist. Cover and infuse for 24 hours in the fridge. Strain the liquid into a sanitized bottle, pressing out liquid from the fruit. Label the bottle with the date and ABV. Store in the fridge for up to 10 days.

Cardamom Black Tea

Makes 1 quart (1 L)

20 grams black tea leaves

1¼ quarts (1.25 L) cold filtered water

5 whole green cardamom pods

Place the tea in a large food-safe container, pour in the water, and add the cardamom. Stir, cover, and infuse in the fridge overnight. Strain the liquid through a mesh sieve into a sanitized bottle, label with the date, and store in the fridge for up to 10 days.

Lavender Cordial

Makes 16 ounces (500 mL)

300 grams superfine or granulated sugar

10 ounces (300 mL) filtered water

3 grams food-grade blue lavender flowers

10 grams citric acid

In a small saucepan, combine the sugar and water. Bring to a slow simmer over medium heat, then immediately remove from the heat. (You don't want it to boil; this is just to dissolve the sugar.) In a heatproof container, using a mallet or muddler, smash the lavender until the essential oils and blue powder release. Pour the sugar water over the flowers, but do not stir; let them infuse their flavor without disrupting the pigment release. After 2 minutes, strain the liquid through a fine-mesh sieve. Whisk in the citric acid until dissolved. Store in a sanitized bottle, labeled with the date, in the fridge for up to 10 days.

————

Raspberry & Coconut Shrub

Makes 10 ounces (300 mL)

5 ounces (150 mL) Toasted Coconut Syrup (page 67)

3½ ounces (90 mL) high-quality raspberry vinegar

2 ounces (60 mL) coconut flower syrup, maple syrup, or raw honey

In a bowl, whisk together the Toasted Coconut Syrup, vinegar, and coconut flower syrup. Store in a sanitized bottle, labeled with the date, in the fridge for up to 10 days.

Saffron Curaçao

Makes 8 ounces (250 mL), 35% ABV

0.25 grams saffron threads

8 ounces (250 mL) orange curaçao or Triple Sec liqueur

Place the saffron in a small jar and press with a muddler a few times to release the oils and pigment. Add the curaçao, close the lid, and shake. Infuse for 24 hours. Strain the liquid into a sanitized bottle and label with the date and ABV. Cover and store indefinitely with your other room-temperature alcohols.

————

Sake with Pineapple

Makes 16 ounces (500 mL), 10% ABV

190 grams chopped pineapple

16 ounces (500 mL) junmai nama sake (see note)

Add the pineapple and sake to a 1-quart (1 L) jar. Fold a paper coffee filter in half and place on top of the pineapple, pressing to soak, to keep the fruit submerged and moist. Cover and infuse for 24 hours in the fridge. Strain the liquid into a sanitized bottle, pressing out liquid from the fruit. Label the bottle with the date and ABV. Store in the fridge for up to 15 days.

Note: For a nonalcoholic version, replace the sake with Seedlip Dry Aperitivo.

Strawberry Beer

Makes 1½ quarts (1.5 L)

110 grams superfine or granulated sugar

1½ quarts (1.5 L) cold filtered water

400 grams strawberries, hulled and halved

2 ounces (60 mL) Pineapple Tepache (page 113) or any other ferment starter

In a large bowl, whisk together the sugar and water until the sugar is dissolved. Add the strawberries to a 2-quart (2 L) jar, preferably with an air lock (see note). Top with the sugar water and tepache (the live, active ferment; a SCOBY is not necessary here). Fold a paper coffee filter in half and place on top of the strawberries, pressing to soak, to keep the fruit submerged and moist. Close the lid. After 5 days, strain the liquid, pressing the strawberries to release the juice, and using a large mesh sieve, filter into smaller bottles with rubber flip tops. Label with the date and store in the fridge for up to 6 months, burping every few days. Reserve some of the SCOBY for a future Strawberry Beer starter.

Note: If you don't have a jar with an air lock, just close the lid and remember to "burp" the jar each day to release the carbon dioxide, a by-product of fermentation.

———

Strawberry Shrub

Makes 16 ounces (500 mL)

200 grams superfine or granulated sugar

7 ounces (200 mL) filtered water

3½ ounces (100 mL) cane vinegar

150 grams strawberries, quartered

3 grams whole black peppercorns

Using an immersion circulator, bring a pot of water to 150°F (65°C) (or use a stem thermometer to hold the temperature on medium heat). In a bowl, whisk together the sugar, water, and vinegar until the sugar is dissolved. Add the strawberries and peppercorns to a heatproof food-safe bag and top with the sugar mixture. Remove the air from the bag, seal, and clip it to the side of the pot, ensuring that the mixture is underwater. Cook for 3 hours. Transfer the bag to an ice bath and let cool. Strain the liquid into a sanitized bottle, reserving the strawberries. Label the bottle with the date and store in the fridge for up to 10 days. Place the strawberries on parchment paper and dry in a dehydrator or a 200°F (93°C) oven overnight, or until bone dry. Let cool, then store in a paper towel–lined airtight container for up to 7 days and use as garnish.

———

Turmeric & Ginger Cordial

Makes 16 ounces (500 mL)

2½-inch (6 cm) piece fresh ginger

1½-inch (4 cm) piece fresh turmeric (see note)

7 grams citric acid

7 grams malic acid

13½ ounces (400 mL) Simple Syrup (page 47)

Set up a juicer. Chop the ginger and turmeric separately into small pieces. Juice and strain the ginger to yield 2½ ounces (75 mL). Juice and strain the turmeric to yield 1 ounce (30 mL). Add the juices to a blender, along with the citric acid, malic acid, and syrup. Blend on medium until the acids are dissolved. Strain the liquid through cheesecloth to microfilter. This syrup should be vibrant and pale orange. Store in a sanitized bottle, labeled with the date, in the fridge for up to 10 days.

Note: When working with turmeric, wear gloves and be aware that it may stain your countertop and utensils. Scrub everything down immediately afterward.

Zero Proof

Nonalcoholic Spritz

Throughout this book are recipes for every occasion and every lifestyle choice. The Zero-Proof movement is a massive step in the drinks industry to create a more inclusive experience for our guests, both at the bar and at home. Every NA vermouth and most of the mise en place recipes in the book will work beautifully whether they're combined with alcoholic or nonalcoholic ingredients. Use them as a template and create your own recipes with flavors that suit the occasion or time of day. Really, just have fun. I never compromise flavor in the absence of alcohol; it's just the opposite—I work harder to create something delicious, innovative, and unique. My friends at Ben Branson, creator/founder of Seedlip and Claire Warner, creator of the Seedlip Aperitivo range,), along with myriad other brands, have done a great job presenting nonalcoholic options, but if you cannot find them or wish to make some of the recipes in this chapter to store in your fridge, I highly encourage it. To get you started, I present the Nonalcoholic Spritz.

Method

To a wineglass filled with ice, add the vermouth, cordial, and bitters. Stir gently with a bar spoon to chill. Add more ice if necessary; it should be right to the top. Fill the glass with NA sparkling wine and sparkling water. Garnish with the citrus wheel.

Serves 1

Area of inspiration: Planet Earth
Inspired by: the Zero-Proof movement

———

2 ounces (60 mL) NA vermouth (pages 235–237)

½ ounce (15 mL) All-Purpose Cordial (page 232)

2 dashes bitters (optional)

2 ounces (60 mL) chilled NA sparkling wine

2 ounces (60 mL) chilled sparkling water (or more as needed)

Garnish: Citrus wheel (orange, lemon, lime, or grapefruit)

Best Person

Dani Tatarin is my person. We're both Taurus women and businessowners, and we're now separated by oceans and continents. Dani lives in Zipolite, Mexico, where she started a mezcal brand, Gota Gorda. For many years, we met up at Tales of the Cocktail for our annual New Orleans reunion. We worked with Lynnette Marrero and Ivy Mix to bring Speed Rack to Canada for the first time in 2015. We were the first two female finalists in World Class Canada, and the first two female winners of *Vancouver* magazine's Bartender of the Year. Dani was the "best person" at Jonathan's and my wedding (she moved from side to side depending on who was speaking at the ceremony). She also founded the Keefer Bar in Vancouver and put it on the international map. Her legacy will continue to fill every glass. This drink is the most appropriate for my Dani memories; it's inspired by international culture, time, and place, and is both beautiful and creative—just as she is. Everything we faced, we faced together, and we overcame challenge after challenge because we had each other.

Method

To a blender, add the syrup, passion fruit puree, lime juice, bitters, rose water, tofu, Golden Milk Powder, xanthan gum, and ice. Blend on high for 15 seconds or until smooth. Pour into one large or two medium rocks glasses. Garnish with the edible flowers and serve with a compostable or reusable straw.

Serves 1 to 2

Area of inspiration: Zipolite, Mexico
Inspired by: the Lassi

———

3 ounces (90 mL) Honey Syrup (page 184)

2 ounces (60 mL) passion fruit puree

¾ ounce (22.5 mL) fresh lime juice

3 dashes spicy aromatic bitters
(like Bittered Sling Moondog Latin)

2 dashes rose water

60 grams silken tofu (extra soft)

5 grams Golden Milk Powder (page 233)

1 gram xanthan gum

6 ice cubes

Garnish: Fresh edible flowers

Buttermylk Cream Soda

ZERO PROOF

Over the last twenty years, bartenders have been trying to push flavors forward and continue to evolve our drinks while taking into consideration that our lifestyles and diets have changed. This cocktail is an evolution of the Buttermilk Cream Soda, using plant-based nut mylks and oils. It is rich and delicious, just as a traditional egg cream would be, but designed for today's need for more dairy-free options. It is inspired by my love of soda fountain culture from the 1950s. Growing up in Toronto in the 1980s, I'm happy I got to experience these drinks before they fell out of fashion for two decades. Around the world, I'm happy to see, and even more happy to taste, the creative and delicious zero-proof drinks that still "drink like a drink." Flavor, story, and ingredients are always paramount over alcohol percentage.

Serves 1

Area of inspiration: Toronto, Ontario
Inspired by: the Egg Cream

———

1½ ounces (45 mL) Buttermylk Cream Syrup (page 232)

1 dash aromatic bitters
(like Bittered Sling Plum & Rootbeer)

5 ounces (150 mL) chilled carbonated water

Garnish: Grated white chocolate, freshly grated nutmeg

Method
To a Collins glass filled with cubed ice, add the syrup and bitters. Stir with a bar spoon to chill. Add more ice if necessary; it should be right to the top. Fill the glass with carbonated water and stir just to combine. Garnish with white chocolate and nutmeg.

Greenish

Hong Kong is filled with so many great bars, from Quinary, owned by my friends Antonio Lai and Charlene Dawes, to the Old Man, J. Boroski, and the Stockton. You'll find others tucked away in the skyscrapers, such as Foxglove (disguised as an umbrella shop), and some hidden in the metro stations underground, like Dr. Fern's Gin Parlor. There are agave bars, like COA in the hills, and iconic bars like the Lobster Bar, Employees Only, and PDT. There are so many spaces and programs to visit and support; it's a jam-packed place with lots to discover. The team I work with in Hong Kong is wonderful, generous and kind, innovative and creative. Cherry Lam springs to mind as the consummate host and an amazing human, but from brand ambassador to bartender to bar owner, the list of great people in Hong Kong is endless, and their generosity radiates. An afternoon tea and dim sum feels traditional, while the evening adventure transpires in a dark skyscraper for a VIP closed-restaurant experience with a super-spicy Szechuan feast of local foods. Midday foot massages between presentations are always welcomed, as is late-night ramen, tucked away in subzero cubicles with a conveyer belt. Each time I have visited Hong Kong it's been humid and hot—it makes one crave refreshing, long cocktails with fresh, tropical flavors. Hong Kong is super innovative and a lot of fun, and while I can hardly wait to go back and taste what's next, I'm excited to make drinks at home with a bit of flare from the region, using some local produce that we have in common back home in Europe.

Serves 1

Area of inspiration: Hong Kong, China
Inspired by: the Collins

———

4 slices cucumber

2 cubes honeydew melon (1-inch/2.5 cm cubes)

1½ ounces (45 mL) White Sand NA Vermouth (page 237)

¾ ounce (22.5 mL) Ginger Shrub (page 93)

¾ ounce (22.5 mL) Simple Syrup (page 47)

½ ounce (15 mL) fresh lime juice

2 dashes celery bitters
(like Bittered Sling Cascade Celery)

2 ounces (60 mL) cold filtered water

Garnish: Honeydew melon peel, bouquet of fresh cilantro, mint, and basil

Method
Place the cucumber and melon in a shaker and press with a muddler to break them up. Fill the shaker with ice and add the vermouth, shrub, syrup, lime juice, and bitters. Using some force, shake hard for 5 seconds. Using a small fine-mesh bar sieve to catch the loose ice chips, double strain into a carbonated drink maker (like the Drinkmate). Add the filtered water and follow the manufacturer's instructions to carbonate. Gently release the pressure and pour into a chilled champagne flute. For the garnish, roll the melon peel around the bouquet of herbs and thread onto a cocktail pick and place across the top of the glass.

Orxata

Horchata (or Orxata, as known in Valencia) is delicious. Full stop, period. Back in 2015, I created a horchata beverage called Panthera for a global competition; it was my "championship" serve should I have made it to the final top six bartenders. The drink was an amalgamation of my experiences with horchata in different regions, trying to bring them together as an expression of world travel. How did a beverage that dates back to the 1300s across Spain, Africa, and eventually Latin America stand the test of time? It was helpful to learn that horchata wasn't originally made from rice at all—it was tiger nuts, a root crop that is intriguing in both flavor and aroma. The African and European recipes are very similar, and reading in the history books about the evolution of the beverage across the pond in the Americas makes horchata seem like a truly international taste of history. The recipe I like best takes a bit from both the old-world and new-world recipes, for a final product made with rice, tiger nut, and coconut milks. It's a delicious beverage served hot or cold, with spicy food or by itself as a refreshing treat on a hot day. I love that it's dairy-free and works with any plant-based mylks you have access to. If you have a rice allergy or aversion, try making it with oat, pea, or hemp mylk along with the tiger nut mylk, though you'll have to adjust the sweetness and spices accordingly. Traveling around the world one cocktail at a time is a brilliant way to celebrate international cultures, and I hope this recipe takes you on your own journey.

Serves 1

Area of inspiration: Spain to Mexico
Inspired by: Horchata

———

6 ounces (175 mL) Horchata (page 234)

2 dashes coffee bitters
(like Bittered Sling Arabica Coffee)

Garnish: Grated cinnamon or a cinnamon stick

Method

Add ice to one shaker and the horchata and bitters to another. Using a loose Hawthorne strainer (one that sits inside the shaker, not on top) to hold the ice back, move the liquid back and forth between the shakers. As you get good at this technique, you'll add a bit more height and aeration. Do this for 10 to 15 seconds, until the liquid is chilled without being overly emulsified or diluted. Strain into a highball glass filled with cubed ice. Garnish with cinnamon.

Note: To turn this zero-proof drink into a mid-proof one, add ¾ ounce (22.5 mL) each rum and amontillado sherry with the horchata.

Pandanus Club

During my 2018 trip to Southeast Asia, I was excited to meet up with legendary bartender and ambassador Rian Assidao. We were in Manila to help train local bartenders. Manila is vast; I couldn't believe the sheer size of the city, and I saw only a fraction of it. Billboards for scotch whisky were everywhere, and dozens of tuk-tuks and scooters whizzed by us at every moment. The bartender who won the local and global community challenge was Lester Ligon. His project was all about providing food and support to regions of the Philippines that house refugee camps and tent cities. Lester developed a delicious fermented rice soda and used it in a mule-style drink with ginger, lime, and sugar. Lester and Rian visited many of the camps and worked with a local chef to turn the spent rice from the soda into useable food (tapai), and a portion of the proceeds from every cocktail supported the same cause. If you've ever thought "Bartenders just make drinks," think again. Bartenders can change the world. This drink, the Pandanus Club, is a riff on the thoughtful and delicious cocktail from Lester's program, in a zero-proof build.

Method

To a shaker filled with cubed ice, add the vermouth, shrub, and bitters. Using some force, shake hard for 5 seconds. Strain into a Collins glass filled with cubed ice. Fill the glass with rice water and stir just to combine. For the garnish, slice a long cheek off the side of a green mango. Cut it into 4 thin slices (1/16 inch/2 mm thick) and thread a cocktail pick through the bottom edge of all the slices together. Fan out from the top once the bottom is secure, and push the pick into the top of the drink.

Serves 1

Area of inspiration: Manila, Philippines
Inspired by: Amazake rice drink

———

1½ ounces (45 mL) White Sand NA Vermouth (page 237)

1½ ounces (45 mL) Mango Shrub (page 234)

2 dashes peach bitters
(like Bittered Sling Clingstone Peach)

5 ounces (150 mL) Carbonated Rice Water (page 233)

Garnish: Green mango fan (see note)

Note: Use a slightly underripe mango, as the flesh and skin are firmer.

Zebra Wine

As an avid student and lover of wine, I had a visit to the Stellenbosch wine region in South Africa on my bucket list. After a massive event in Cape Town, 60 other bartenders and I had a chance to visit this legendary region. I have always been fascinated with Pinotage, a hybrid of Pinot Noir and Cinsault grapes known worldwide as one of the quintessential flavors of South Africa's wine portfolio. The region produces many delicious grapes, including epic Chardonnay, Chenin Blanc, Muscat, and Bordeaux red varietals like Cabernet Sauvignon, Merlot, and Cabernet Franc. Even more interesting than the table wines is Caperitif white vermouth, made from Chenin Blanc and botanicals native to South Africa. I had used it in one of my cocktail presentations earlier that week, grabbing a bottle from a local shop as we got off the plane. In the afternoon, as we baked in the sun with a crisp glass of white wine in hand, we watched at a distance as zebras and other grazing animals pranced around in neighboring fields. It was like we were in a dream. This drink captures some of the unique flavors we enjoyed that day and commemorates how lucky we were to be together at that moment. Enjoy it with antipasti, including biltong (South African beef jerky) if you can get it.

Method

Add cubed ice to a Lewis bag and smash into chips with a mallet. Fill a Collins glass halfway with crushed ice and add the tea, vermouth, shrub, and bitters. Stir gently with a bar spoon to chill. Add more crushed ice to fill right to the top. Garnish with the grated coffee bean, strawberry, and orange wheel. Serve with a long, wide reusable or compostable straw.

Serves 1

Area of inspiration: Stellenbosch, South Africa
Inspired by: the Americano

———

3 ounces (90 mL) Cascara Tea (page 233) or brewed rooibos tea

2 ounces (60 mL) Rhythmic Red NA Vermouth (page 236)

1 ounce (30 mL) Strawberry Shrub (page 215)

1 dash coffee bitters
(like Bittered Sling Arabica Coffee)

Garnish: Grated coffee bean, strawberry (fresh or dehydrated), dehydrated orange wheel

Mise en Place Recipes

All-Purpose Cordial

Makes 16 ounces (500 mL)

300 grams superfine or granulated sugar

5 grams citric acid

5 grams tartaric acid

5 grams malic acid

Pinch kosher salt

10 ounces (300 mL) filtered water

In a bowl, whisk together the sugar, acids, salt, and water until the sugar is dissolved. Store in a sanitized bottle, labeled with the date, in the fridge for up to 10 days.

Buttermylk Cream Syrup

Makes 16 ounces (500 mL)

¼ vanilla bean

300 grams superfine or granulated sugar

20 grams gum arabic powder

7 ounces (200 mL) coconut milk

3½ ounces (100 mL) warm filtered water

10 grams lactic acid

2 grams kosher salt

1 drop vanilla essential oil (see note)

Split the vanilla bean and scrape out the seeds, reserving the bean to make vanilla extract (see note, page 132). To a blender, add the sugar, gum arabic, coconut milk, and warm water. With the motor running, through the hole in the top, add the vanilla seeds, lactic acid, salt, and essential oil. Blend on medium until the sugar is dissolved. Strain the liquid through a mesh sieve into a sanitized bottle, label with the date, and store in the fridge for up to 10 days.

Note: Use only natural, pure vanilla essential oil (no carrier oils) and use a pipette to add a single drop. The oil is highly concentrated, and 1 drop is more than enough to aromatize. Store essential oils in the fridge in sealed containers.

Cascara Tea

Makes 1 quart (1 L)

1 quart (1 L) filtered water

20 grams cascara (dried coffee husks)

Bring the water to a slow simmer, then turn off the heat (do not boil). Add the cascara to a heatproof container and pour in the hot water. Infuse for 15 minutes. Strain the liquid through a mesh sieve and let cool completely. Store in a sanitized bottle, labeled with the date, in the fridge for up to 10 days. Recarbonate as needed.

―――

Carbonated Rice Water

Makes 1¼ quarts (1.25 L)

250 grams koshihikari (sushi-grade) white rice, rinsed

1¼ quarts (1.25 L) cold filtered water

Add the rice to a food-safe container and pour in the water. Stir, cover, and infuse for 1 hour. Strain the liquid through a mesh sieve, reserving the rice for cooking. Add the liquid to a carbonated drink maker (like the Drinkmate) and follow the manufacturer's instructions to carbonate. Store in a sanitized bottle, labeled with the date, in the fridge for up to 10 days. Recarbonate as needed.

Golden Milk Powder

Makes 90 grams

30 grams confectioners' sugar

30 grams coconut cream powder

10 grams ground turmeric

7.5 grams ground ginger

5 grams grated cinnamon

3 grams freshly ground black pepper

2 grams grated nutmeg

0.5 gram ground cloves

Pinch fine pink salt

Add all ingredients to a clean spice mill and grind until fine and well combined, about 1 minute. Sift through a fine-mesh sieve into a small jar and store in the pantry for up to 1 month.

―――

Grapefruit & Cardamom Oleo Syrup

Makes 16 ounces (500 mL)

250 grams superfine or granulated sugar

115 grams grapefruit peels (from about 2 large grapefruits)

4 green cardamom pods (about 1 gram), smashed

8 ounces (250 mL) water

Add the sugar, grapefruit peels, and cardamom to an airtight container and press with a muddler. Cover and let stand for 24 hours. The next day, transfer the mixture to a blender, along with the water. Blend on medium until the sugar is dissolved. Strain the liquid through a mesh sieve, then through cheesecloth to microfilter. Store in a sanitized bottle, labeled with the date, in the fridge for up to 10 days.

Horchata

Makes 2 quarts (2 L)

2 cinnamon sticks

24 ounces (750 mL) tiger nut milk

24 ounces (750 mL) rice milk

7 ounces (200 mL) coconut milk

12 ounces (375 mL) Simple Syrup (page 47)

⅓ ounce (10 mL) chocolate bitters (like Bittered Sling Malagasy Chocolate)

Place the cinnamon sticks in a food-safe container with a tight-fitting lid and add the plant mylks. Stir, cover, and refrigerate for 24 hours. In two batches, transfer the mixture (including the cinnamon sticks) to a blender and blend on medium-high for 30 seconds. Strain through a mesh sieve, and repeat if necessary. Wash out the blender pitcher. In two batches, return the mylk mixture to the blender and add half each of the syrup and bitters to each batch. Blend again on medium speed. Strain through cheesecloth to microfilter. Store in sanitized bottles, labeled with the date, in the fridge for up to 10 days. Shake or stir before using.

Mango Shrub

Makes 13 ounces (400 mL)

150 grams superfine or granulated sugar

5 ounces (150 mL) mango juice

5 ounces (150 mL) cane vinegar

To a blender, add the sugar, mango juice, and vinegar. Blend on medium until the sugar is dissolved. Strain the liquid through a mesh sieve into a sanitized bottle, label with the date, and store in the fridge for up to 10 days.

Nonalcoholic & Alcoholic Vermouths

Nonalcoholic Vermouths

All of these nonalcoholic (NA) vermouths are named for colors rather than specific flavors, and they are all made the same way, listed below in a Master Method. Each one becomes a base for the 18% alcoholic vermouths that follow.

Master Method

Use this method for all NA vermouths. Using an immersion circulator, bring a pot of water to 195°F (90°C) (or use a stem thermometer to hold the temperature on medium-high heat). In a bowl, whisk together the sugar(s), water, and NA wine until the sugar is dissolved. Add the remaining ingredients to a heatproof food-safe bag and top with the liquid mixture. Remove the air from the bag, seal, and clip it to the side of the pot, ensuring that the mixture is underwater. Cook for 1½ hours. Transfer the bag to an ice bath and let cool. Strain into a sanitized bottle, label with the date, and store in the fridge for up to 1 month.

Black Sand NA Vermouth

Makes 16 ounces (500 mL)

100 grams superfine or granulated sugar

80 grams dark brown sugar

20 grams blackstrap molasses

8 ounces (250 mL) filtered water

8 ounces (250 mL) nonalcoholic red wine (like Grenache)

4 whole cloves

130 grams sliced frozen banana

40 grams dried figs

12.5 grams orange peels

3.5 grams cacao nibs

3.5 grams citric acid

2 grams black tea leaves

2 grams burdock root

2 grams dried chicory root, toasted

2 grams American oak chips

1 gram allspice berries

1 gram black cardamom pods, smashed

1 gram cinnamon stick

1 gram kosher salt

¼ ounce (7.5 mL) cinchona bark tincture

Calypso Coral NA Vermouth

Makes 16 ounces (500 mL)

100 grams superfine or granulated sugar

8 ounces (250 mL) filtered water

8 ounces (250 mL) nonalcoholic rosé wine (like Syrah)

50 grams fresh rhubarb, chopped

10 grams dried strawberries

6 grams grapefruit peels

6 grams dried apricots, chopped

5 grams fresh ginger (about a 1-inch/2.5 cm piece), thinly sliced

5 grams preserved lemon peels, chopped

3.5 grams dried edible roses

3.5 grams citric acid

2 grams dried edible marigold flowers (available online)

2 grams dried edible peony flowers

2 grams dried food-grade lavender

1 gram wormwood

1 gram kosher salt

¼ ounce (7.5 mL) cinchona bark tincture

Rhythmic Red NA Vermouth

Makes 16 ounces (500 mL)

100 grams superfine or granulated sugar

8 ounces (250 mL) filtered water

8 ounces (250 mL) nonalcoholic red wine (like Grenache)

2 whole cloves

½ star anise pod

½ guajillo chili pepper (savory, not spicy)

15 grams dried cranberries

15 grams golden raisins

12.5 grams dried orange peels

5 grams sun-dried tomatoes

3.5 grams citric acid

3 grams gentian root

2 grams dried edible hibiscus flowers

1.5 grams dried chicory root, toasted

1 gram annatto seeds

1 gram licorice root

1 gram kosher salt

¼ ounce (7.5 mL) cinchona bark tincture

Tawny Orange NA Vermouth

Makes 16 ounces (500 mL)

80 grams creamed raw white honey

20 grams superfine or granulated sugar

8 ounces (250 mL) filtered water

8 ounces (250 mL) nonalcoholic white wine (like Muscat)

6 slices fresh turmeric

15 grams green olives (about 10), pitted and sliced

12.5 grams dried bitter orange peels

12.5 grams dried sweet orange peels

10 grams pineapple, cubed

7 grams dried apricots, chopped

5 grams preserved lemon peels, chopped

3.5 grams citric acid

3 grams fresh lemongrass, chopped

2 grams rooibos tea leaves

2 grams sherry oak chips

1 gram green cardamom pods, smashed

1 gram kosher salt

¼ ounce (7.5 mL) cinchona bark tincture

White Sand NA Vermouth

Makes 16 ounces (500 mL)

100 grams superfine or granulated sugar

8 ounces (250 mL) coconut water

8 ounces (250 mL) nonalcoholic white wine (like Muscat)

20 grams canned lychee fruit, rinsed and chopped

12 grams unsweetened coconut flakes, toasted

6 grams dried lemon peels

5 grams fresh lemongrass, chopped

3.5 grams citric acid

2 grams marshmallow root

2 grams whole dried apple rings

2 grams green cardamom pods, smashed

2 grams dandelion root

2 grams American oak chips

1 gram tonka bean, crushed

2 grams cinnamon stick (about 2 inches/5 cm)

1 gram kosher salt

¼ ounce (7.5 mL) cinchona bark tincture

18% Alcoholic Vermouths

All of these 18% vermouths are named for colors rather than specific flavors, and they are all made the same way, listed below in a Master Method.

Master Method

Add all ingredients to a small bowl and stir to combine. Store in a sanitized bottle, labeled with the date and ABV, in the fridge for up to 3 months.

——

Green Cameo Vermouth

Makes 8½ ounces (265 mL)

2 ounces (60 mL) Tawny Orange NA Vermouth (page 237)

2 ounces (60 mL) fino sherry

2 ounces (60 mL) 100% agave blanco tequila

2 ounces (60 mL) Lemongrass & Lime Leaf Syrup (page 93)

¼ ounce (7.5 mL) fresh ginger juice

1 teaspoon (5 mL) celery bitters (like Bittered Sling Cascade Celery)

1 teaspoon (5 mL) grapefruit bitters (like Bittered Sling Grapefruit & Hops)

——

Infrared Red Vermouth

Makes 9¾ ounces (295 mL)

4½ ounces (140 mL) Rhythmic Red NA Vermouth (page 236)

3¾ ounces (115 mL) vodka

1½ ounces (45 mL) Simple Syrup (page 47)

Mellow Yellow Vermouth

Makes 8¼ ounces (255 mL)

4½ ounces (140 mL) White Sand NA Vermouth (page 237)

2¾ ounces (85 mL) Tanqueray No. Ten gin

1 ounce (30 mL) Grapefruit & Cardamom Oleo Syrup (page 233)

——

Nebula Pink Vermouth

Makes 9¾ ounces (295 mL)

4½ ounces (140 mL) Calypso Coral NA Vermouth (page 236)

3¾ ounces (115 mL) London dry gin

1½ ounces (45 mL) Simple Syrup (page 47)

——

Red Leather Vermouth

Makes 9¾ ounces (295 mL)

4½ ounces (140 mL) Rhythmic Red NA Vermouth (page 236)

2¾ ounces (85 mL) 100% agave blanco tequila

1½ ounces (45 mL) Simple Syrup (page 47)

1 ounce (30 mL) Espadín mezcal

Singularity Dark Vermouth

Makes 9¾ ounces (295 mL)

4½ ounces (140 mL) Black Sand NA Vermouth (page 235)

3¾ ounces (115 mL) dark rum

1½ ounces (45 mL) Simple Syrup (page 47)

———

Solar Flare Orange Vermouth

Makes 9¾ ounces (295 mL)

4½ ounces (140 mL) Tawny Orange NA Vermouth (page 237)

3¾ ounces (115 mL) London dry gin

1½ ounces (45 mL) Simple Syrup (page 47)

———

Starlight White Vermouth

Makes 9¾ ounces (295 mL)

4½ ounces (140 mL) White Sand NA Vermouth (page 237)

3¾ ounces (115 mL) white rum

1½ ounces (45 mL) Simple Syrup (page 47)

ACKNOWLEDGMENTS

We are born with gifts, and no two people are the same. We evolve with hard work to develop our gifts, which become useful skills not only in the world at large, but in the world we create for ourselves. Along the way, many people come into our lives to give advice, guidance, or an opinion, or simply to listen. I am truly blessed to have had a wonderful network, both in the present and in the past, helping me build the world of tomorrow. Thank you to each person referenced in the book; you've each played a role in my life, and there are never enough pages to mention everyone.

Some additional folks helped bring this project to life (in no particular order): the Bender Food Service Team; Spiegelau Germany; Derek Hoogstra of Cascadia Tableware; the teams at the Four Seasons Vancouver, Whistler, and San Francisco; the Tales of the Cocktail, Bacardi, Campari, Diageo, Beam Suntory, Brown-Forman, Pernod-Ricard, LVMH, and Christopher Stewart teams; the incredibly talented and inspirational bartending and culinary communities in Toronto and Vancouver; international friends and colleagues I've met over years of extensive travel around the world; the immediate and extended Mote, Dolgy, and Chovancek families; my mentors Linda Mote and Anya Haarhoff; my husband, Jonathan; and my dachshund, Moondog Longer Mocho. Also all the #bitterbabes, importers, partners, and distributors who make each day as an entrepreneur so fulfilling. Huge thanks to Carole Morton, Shelley McArthur, Johnathon Vaughn Strebly and the Epix team, Sherrill Sirrs, Rodney Goodchild, Tyler and Tony Dyck, Amorita Adair, Sherri Zielinski, and Luca Citton for having our backs. And thanks to my co-author, James O. Fraioli.

To the Penguin Random House Canada team: Kristin Cochrane, president and CEO; Robert McCullough, publisher; Zoe Maslow (the MVP), editor; Lindsay Paterson, editorial director; Terri Nimmo, book designer; Carla Kean, director of production; and Susan Burns, managing editor. Thank you all.

INDEX

Subject Index

A

ABV. *See* alcohol by volume
agave spirits. *See also* tequila
  about, 10
alcohol by volume, 21
All-Purpose Cordial, 232
All-Purpose Flower, 28
All-Purpose Flower Cordial, 46
almonds: Orgeat, 47
aloe vera juice: Century Plant, 42
amari, about, 11
apple: Chicha Morada Mix, 67
apple cider vinegar: The
    Unclimbable, 173
Apple Honey Shrub, 156
apple juice: Apple Honey Shrub, 156
Apple Syrup, 66
Apple-ation, 50
aquavit, about, 11
Autumn & Eve, 70

B

Babka Orgeat, 212
Bagel Shrub, 156
Bajan Apéritif, 188
Bajan Spice Syrup, 212
Balsam Fir Spray, 184
Banana Tepache, 213
bananas
    Black Sand NA Vermouth, 235
    Caramelized Banana Pyramid,
    119
    Caramelized Banana Syrup, 92
Basil Cordial, 46
beets: Rainbow Beet Cordial, 159
Best Person, 221
Betacillin, 174
Bitter Brain Freeze, 106
bitters, about, 13
Black Forest, 208
Black Sand NA Vermouth, 235
Blood Orange Grenadine, 213

blueberry purée: Dancing Queen,
    128
Boréal Cordial, 66
Bottleshock, 191
brandy, about, 10
butter: Buttered Oolong Toddy,
    109
Buttermylk Cream Soda, 222
Buttermylk Cream Syrup, 232

C

California Citrus Cordial, 92
Calypso Coral NA Vermouth, 236
Camp Pal-o-Mine, 98
cane vinegar
    Apple Honey Shrub, 156
    Bagel Shrub, 156
    Honey Cup Shrub, 158
    Mango Shrub, 234
Cantaloupe Chardonnay, 213
Caramelized Banana Pyramid, 119
Caramelized Banana Syrup, 92
Carbonated Rice Water, 233
cardamom
    Cardamom Black Tea, 213
    Cardamom Curaçao, 46
    Déjà Brew, 200
    Grapefruit & Cardamom Oleo
        Syrup, 233
    Strong Cardamom Coffee, 133
Cardamom Curaçao, 46
carrot juice: Betacillin, 174
carrots: Denman Street Caesar
    Mix, 157
cascara
    Cascara Tea, 233
    Kola Nut & Cascara Syrup, 132
Cascara Tea, 233
celery
    Celery Cordial, 47
    Denman Street Caesar Mix, 157
Celery Cordial, 47
Century Plant, 42
Champagne Josephine, 192

champagne vinegar: White Grape
    Cordial, 133
Chartreuse Milkshake, 101
Cherry Cola Cordial, 184
Chicha Morada Mix, 67
Chicka Cherry Cola, 162
cocktails, designing, 23–25
coconut cream: Late-Night
    Ramos, 85
coconut cream powder: Golden
    Milk Powder, 233
coconut flakes
    Toasted Coconut Syrup, 67
    White Sand NA Vermouth, 237
coconut flower nectar: Peak Me
    Up, 119
coconut flower syrup
    Iberian Apéritif, 203
    Raspberry & Coconut Shrub,
    214
coconut milk
    Buttermylk Cream Syrup, 232
    Horchata, 234
    Milk Syrup, 132
Coconut Vodka with Roses, 112
coconut water
    Bitter Brain Freeze, 106
    Bottleshock, 191
    Jugo de Selva, 61
    White Sand NA Vermouth, 237
coffee
    Peak Me Up, 119
    Stout, Stout, Let It All Out, 177
    Strong Cardamom Coffee, 133
Cola Flower Water, 185
Cold as Rice, 196
confectioners' sugar: Golden Milk
    Powder, 233
cordials. *See also* syrups
    All-Purpose Flower Cordial, 46
    Basil Cordial, 46
    Boréal Cordial, 66
    California Citrus Cordial, 92
    Cardamom Curaçao, 46

Celery Cordial, 47
Cherry Cola Cordial, 184
Jaffa Orange Crush Cordial, 185
Orgeat, 47
Pomelo Cordial, 158
Pumpkin Seed Orgeat, 47
Rainbow Beet Cordial, 159
Root Beer Cordial, 112
Rose & Raspberry Cordial, 94
White Grape Cordial, 133
corn: Chicha Morada Mix, 67
Cosmonauts 1 & 2, 136
cranberries: Rhythmic Red NA
        Vermouth, 236
cranberry juice, sugar-free:
        Cosmonauts 1 & 2, 136
cucumber
        Denman Street Caesar Mix, 157
        Greenish, 225

D
Daiquirita, 31
Dancing Queen, 128
Déjà Brew, 200
Denman Street Caesar Mix, 157
Donostia Askatuta, 57
Double-Double Caesar, 139

E
eaux de vies, about, 10
eggs
        Chartreuse Milkshake, 101
        Donostia Askatuta, 57
        Electric Avenue, 72–73
        Gin & Symphonic, 74
        Grand Palace, 144
        The Kasbah, 82
        Late-Night Ramos, 85
        Open Sesame, 204
        Pasteis de Nata, 65
        Pumpkin Spice Ice Cream, 94
        Sour Roses, 102
Electric Avenue, 72–73
Estonian Finnisher, 140
Everything Bagel Spice, 157

F
Family Affair, 32

figs: Black Sand NA Vermouth, 235
Flora Fashion, 116

G
Genever, 10–11. *See also* gin
Georgia on My Mind, 143
gin, about, 10–11
Gin & Symphonic, 74
ginger
        Cherry Cola Cordial, 184
        Ginger Shrub, 93
        Green Cameo Vermouth, 238
        Jaffa Orange Crush Cordial, 185
        Tula Gingerbread Syrup, 95
        Turmeric & Ginger Cordial, 215
ginger beer
        Century Plant, 42
        Seven Mile Mule, 150
Ginger Shrub, 93
Gin-Gin Donkey Kong, 77
Glacial Snout, 180
Golden Milk Powder, 233
Gondwana, 35
Good Vibes Only, 58
Grand Palace, 144
Grapefruit & Cardamom Oleo
        Syrup, 233
grapefruit juice
        California Citrus Cordial, 92
        24 Hours of Darkness, 211
Green Cameo Vermouth, 238
green tea kombucha: Kale & Nori,
        81
Greenish, 225
guarana soda: São Paulo Swizzle,
        124

H
Here Comes the Sun, 147
Hibiscus Agua Fresca, 132
Hibiscus Syrup, 112
Historically Famous, 78
honey
        Apple Honey Shrub, 156
        Buttered Oolong Toddy, 109
        Honey Cup Shrub, 158
        Tawny Orange NA Vermouth, 237
Honey Cup Shrub, 158

Honey Syrup, 185
Horchata, 234

I
Iberian Apéritif, 203
ice cream, coconut
        Bitter Brain Freeze, 106
        Déjà Brew, 200
ice cream: Pumpkin Spice Ice
        Cream, 94
Infrared Red Vermouth, 238
ingredients, recommended, 14–15
Instant Crush, 45
Irish gorse syrup: Apple-ation, 50
It's Jammy, 195

J
Jaffa Orange Crush Cordial, 185
jalapeño peppers: Family Affair, 32
Jugo de Selva, 61
Juicy Fruit, 127

K
Kale & Nori, 81
The Kasbah, 82
Kentucky Crush, 166
Kola Nut & Cascara Syrup, 132
kola nuts: Kola Nut & Cascara
        Syrup, 132
kombucha: Estonian Finnisher,
        140
Kumquat Shrub, 113

L
Late-Night Ramos, 85
Lavender Cordial, 214
Lavender Syrup, 67
lemon brine
        Gin & Symphonic, 74
        Smallage, Biggish, 91
lemon juice
        Bagel Shrub, 156
        Betacillin, 174
        California Citrus Cordial, 92
        Cosmonauts 1 & 2, 136
        Daiquirita, 31
        Dancing Queen, 128
        Denman Street Caesar Mix, 157

Electric Avenue, 72–73
Gin-Gin Donkey Kong, 77
Glacial Snout, 180
Grand Palace, 144
Late-Night Ramos, 85
Pasteis de Nata, 65
24 Hours of Darkness, 211
Lemongrass & Lime Leaf Syrup, 93
Liberation, 53
lime juice
    Autumn & Eve, 70
    Best Person, 221
    California Citrus Cordial, 92
    Camp Pal-o-Mine, 98
    Chartreuse Milkshake, 101
    Daiquirita, 31
    Greenish, 225
    Jugo de Selva, 61
    Late-Night Ramos, 85
    Mercado Mai Thai, 36
    São Paulo Swizzle, 124
    Sour Roses, 102
    Yonge Street, 41
lime: Juicy Fruit, 127
lime leaves: Lemongrass & Lime
    Leaf Syrup, 93
liqueurs, about, 11, 13
Loup-Garou, 183
lychee fruit: White Sand NA
    Vermouth, 237
lychee puree: Cold as Rice, 196

M
mango juice: Mango Shrub, 234
Mango Shrub, 234
maple syrup
    Boréal Cordial, 66
    Déjà Brew, 200
    One Below, 169
    Root Beer Cordial, 112
    The Unclimbable, 173
Marigold Wine, 157
marmalade: Here Comes the Sun,
    147
Mellow Yellow Vermouth, 238
melon: Greenish, 225
Mercado Mai Thai, 36

Miami Stucco Machine, 131
Milk Syrup, 132
Miraflores Chicha Morada, 62
molasses, blackstrap
    Black Sand NA Vermouth, 235
    Root Beer Cordial, 112
    Stout, Stout, Let It All Out, 177

N
Nebula Pink Vermouth, 238
Nonalcoholic Spritz, 218
nonalcoholic (NA) vermouths
    Black Sand NA Vermouth, 235
    Calypso Coral NA Vermouth,
        236
    Master Method, 235

O
olives: Smoked Olives, 203
One Below, 169
Open Sesame, 204
Orange Amargo, 113
orange juice
    All-Purpose Flower, 28
    California Citrus Cordial, 92
    Chartreuse Milkshake, 101
    Jaffa Orange Crush Cordial, 185
    Mercado Mai Thai, 36
orange marmalade: Here Comes
    the Sun, 147
oranges
    Blood Orange Grenadine, 213
    Jaffa Orange Crush Cordial, 185
Orgeat, 47
Orxata, 226

P
Pandanus Club, 229
passion fruit: Juicy Fruit, 127
passion fruit powder: Grand
    Palace, 144
passion fruit puree: Best Person,
    221
Pasteis de Nata, 65
Peak Me Up, 119
peanut butter, powdered: Electric
    Avenue, 72–73
Peaskeeper, 199

pickle brine: We're Pickle People,
    154
pineapple
    Pineaple Tepache, 113
    Sake with Pineapple, 214
pineapple juice
    Autumn & Eve, 70
    Yonge Street, 41
pineapple peels: Chicha Morada
    Mix, 67
Pineapple Tepache, 113
Polar Vortex, 170
Pomelo Cordial, 158
proof, about, 21
pumpkin purée: Pumpkin Spice Ice
    Cream, 94
Pumpkin Seed Orgeat, 47
Pumpkin Spice Ice Cream, 94

Q
quince: Chicha Morada Mix, 67
Quite Apeeling, 207

R
Rainbow Beet Cordial, 159
raisins
    Babka Orgeat, 212
    Rhythmic Red NA Vermouth,
        236
raspberries: Rose & Raspberry
    Cordial, 94
Raspberry & Coconut Shrub, 214
raspberry vinegar: Raspberry &
    Coconut Shrub, 214
Red Leather Vermouth, 238
rhubarb: Calypso Coral NA
    Vermouth, 236
Rhythmic Red NA Vermouth, 236
rice: Carbonated Rice Water, 233
rice milk: Horchata, 234
Rose & Raspberry Cordial, 94
Rosemary Syrup, 185
roses, edible
    Coconut Vodka with Roses, 112
    Jaffa Orange Crush Cordial, 185
    Rose & Raspberry Cordial, 94
rum, about, 11

S

Saffron Curaçao, 214
sake, about, 13
Sake with Pineapple, 214
Saline Solution, 95
São Paulo Swizzle, 124
Sea Basin Bitter, 95
Sea Basin Sbagliato, 88
Seedlip Garden 108
sesame seeds
    Babka Orgeat, 212
    Everything Bagel Spice, 157
Seven Mile Mule, 150
sherry, about, 13
shrubs
    Apple Honey Shrub, 156
    Bagel Shrub, 156
    Ginger Shrub, 93
    Honey Cup Shrub, 158
    Kumquat Shrub, 113
    Mango Shrub, 234
    Raspberry & Coconut Shrub,
        214
    Strawberry Shrub, 215
Simple Syrup, 47
Singularity Dark Vermouth, 239
Smallage, Biggish, 91
Smoked Olives, 203
Solar Flare Orange Vermouth, 239
Sour Roses, 102
soy sauce
    Cold as Rice, 196
    Denman Street Caesar Mix, 157
Spiced Rum, 133
Starlight White Vermouth, 239
Stout, Stout, Let It All Out, 177
strawberries
    Calypso Coral NA Vermouth, 236
    Strawberry Beer, 215
    Strawberry Shrub, 215
Strong Cardamom Coffee, 133
syrups
    Apple Syrup, 66
    Bajan Spice Syrup, 212
    Caramelized Banana Syrup, 92

Ginger Shrub, 93
Grapefruit & Cardamom Oleo
    Syrup, 233
Hibiscus Syrup, 112
Honey Syrup, 185
Kola Nut & Cascara Syrup, 132
Lavender Syrup, 67
Lemongrass & Lime Leaf
    Syrup, 93
Milk Syrup, 132
Rosemary Syrup, 185
Simple Syrup, 47
Tula Gingerbread Syrup, 95
Vanilla Syrup, 159

T

tangerine: Juicy Fruit, 127
Tawny Orange NA Vermouth, 237
tea, black
    Cardamom Black Tea, 213
    Déjà Brew, 200
    Donostia Askatuta, 57
    Gin-Gin Donkey Kong, 77
    Kentucky Crush, 166
tea, oolong: Buttered Oolong
    Toddy, 109
tepache: Pineapple Tepache, 113
tequila, about, 10
tiger nut milk: Horchata, 234
Tinto Naranja, 110
Toasted Coconut Syrup, 67
tofu: Best Person, 221
tomatoes: Denman Street Caesar
    Mix, 157
tools and equipment, 9, 16–20
Tula Gingerbread Syrup, 95
Turmeric & Ginger Cordial, 215
24 Hours of Darkness, 211

U

The Unclimbable, 173

V

Vanilla Syrup, 159
Varuna Coffee, 120

verjuice
    It's Jammy, 195
    White Grape Cordial, 133
vermouth, about, 13
Vieux Boréal, 54
vinegar, apple cider: The
    Unclimbable, 173
vinegar, cane
    Apple Honey Shrub, 156
    Bagel Shrub, 156
    Honey Cup Shrub, 158
    Mango Shrub, 234
    Strawberry Shrub, 215
vinegar, champagne: White Grape
    Cordial, 133
vinegar, raspberry: Raspberry &
    Coconut Shrub, 214
vodka, about, 11
Volcan de Masaya, 123

W

Wanna-Bee, 153
We're Pickle People, 154
Westphalia, 105
whiskey, about, 12
White Grape Cordial, 133
White Sand NA Vermouth, 237
wine, about, 13
wine, red NA
    Rhythmic Red NA Vermouth,
        236
wine, white NA
    Tawny Orange NA Vermouth,
        237
    White Sand NA Vermouth, 237

X

xanthan gum, Late-Night Ramos,
    85

Y

Yonge Street, 41

Z

Zebra Wine, 230

Recipes by Liquor Type

A

amaretto
Déjà Brew, 200
Good Vibes Only, 58
amaro. *See also* Fernet-Branca
Buttered Oolong Toddy, 109
Volcan de Masaya, 123
apple brandy
Apple-ation, 50
Boréal Cordial, 65
Liberation, 53
Vieux Boréal, 54
apple cider: The Unclimbable, 173
apricot liqueur: Historically
Famous, 78
aquavit
Smallage, Biggish, 91
24 Hours of Darkness, 211
We're Pickle People, 154

B

banana liqueur: Peak Me Up, 119
beer, saison: Century Pant, 42
bitters, aromatic
Best Person, 221
Bitter Brain Freeze, 106
Buttermylk Cream Soda, 222
Chicka Cherry Cola, 162
Double-Double Caesar, 139
Family Affair, 32
Instant Crush, 45
Loup-Garou, 183
Mercado Mai Thai, 36
Miraflores Chicha Morada, 62
Peak Me Up, 119
Pumpkin Spice Ice Cream, 94
Stout, Stout, Let It All Out, 177
Yonge Street, 41
bitters, celery
Apple-ation, 50
Champagne Josephine, 192
Estonian Finnisher, 140
Glacial Snout, 180
Green Cameo Vermouth, 238
Greenish, 225
Liberation, 53

Loup-Garou, 183
Smallage, Biggish, 91
bitters, cherry
Apple-ation, 50
Betacillin, 174
Georgia on My Mind, 143
It's Jammy, 195
Peaskeeper, 199
Sour Roses, 102
Vieux Boréal, 54
Volcan de Masaya, 123
bitters, chocolate
Autumn & Eve, 70
Black Forest, 208
Buttered Oolong Toddy, 109
Chartreuse Milkshake, 101
Dancing Queen, 128
Déjà Brew, 200
Electric Avenue, 72–73
Flora Fashion, 116
Grand Palace, 144
Horchata, 234
One Below, 169
Pasteis de Nata, 65
bitters, coffee
Gin-Gin Donkey Kong, 77
Open Sesame, 204
Orxata, 226
São Paulo Swizzle, 124
Zebra Wine, 230
bitters, grapefruit
Green Cameo Vermouth, 238
Here Comes the Sun, 147
Kale & Nori, 81
Sea Basin Bitter, 95
Seven Mile Mule, 150
24 Hours of Darkness, 211
The Unclimbable, 173
Wanna-Bee, 153
bitters, lemon
Bottleshock, 191
Gin & Symphonic, 74
Iberian Apéritif, 203
The Kasbah, 82
Polar Vortex, 170
Westphalia, 105
bitters, orange
All-Purpose Flower, 28

Bajan Apéritif, 188
Gondwana, 35
Historically Famous, 78
Orange Amargo, 113
Smallage, Biggish, 91
Tinto Naranja, 110
We're Pickle People, 154
bitters, peach
Donostia Askatuta, 57
Good Vibes Only, 58
Jugo de Selva, 61
Kentucky Crush, 166
Miami Stucco Machine, 131
Pandanus Club, 229
Quite Apeeling, 207
bourbon
Bitter Brain Freeze, 106
Chicka Cherry Cola, 162
Déjà Brew, 200
Kentucky Crush, 166
brandy. *See also* apple brandy;
cognac; pisco brandy
Apple-ation, 50
Donostia Askatuta, 57
Iberian Apéritif, 203
It's Jammy, 195

C

cachaça
Juicy Fruit, 127
São Paulo Swizzle, 124
Calvados. *See* apple brandy
Campari
Camp Pal-o-Mine, 98
Sour Roses, 102
Canadian whisky: Vieux Boréal,
54
champagne: Champagne
Josephine, 192
Chartreuse, green: Chartreuse
Milkshake, 101
Chartreuse, yellow: Glacial Snout,
180
cherry liqueur: Volcan de Masaya,
123
coconut liqueur
Bottleshock, 191
Grand Palace, 144

cognac
    Good Vibes Only, 58
    Pasteis de Nata, 65
crème de cacao
    Chartreuse Milkshake, 101
    Dancing Queen, 128
    Electric Avenue, 72–73
crème de cassis: Instant Crush, 45
curaçao
    Cadamom Curaçao, 46
    Gondwana, 35
    Yonge Street, 41
curaçao, orange: Saffron Curaçao,
    214

E

eau de vie. See fraise eau de vie;
    framboise eau de vie; kirsch
    eau de vie; pear eau de vie;
    plum eau de vie; quince
    eau de vie

F

Fernet-Branca
    Bitter Brain Freeze, 106
    Instant Crush, 45
fraise eau de vie: Electric Avenue,
    72–73
framboise eau de vie: Champagne
    Josephine, 192

G

Genever: Historically Famous, 78
gin
    Autumn & Eve, 70
    Champagne Josephine, 192
    Chartreuse Milkshake, 101
    Electric Avenue, 72–73
    Gin-Gin Donkey Kong, 77
    Gin & Symphonic, 74
    Kale & Nori, 81
    The Kasbah, 82
    Mellow Yellow Vermouth, 238
    Nebula Pink Vermouth, 238
    Sea Basin Sbagliato, 88
    Smallage, Biggish, 91
    Solar Flare Orange Vermouth,
        239

Westphalia, 105
ginger liqueur: Betacillin, 174
Guinness stout: Stout, Stout, Let It
    All Out, 177

I

Irish whiskey: Apple-ation, 50

J

Jägermeister: Westphalia, 105

K

kirsch eau de vie: Black Forest,
    208

L

liqueur. See also cherry liqueur;
    coconut liqueur; ginger
    liqueur
liqueur, white bitter: Liberation,
    53

M

Madeira: Quite Apeeling, 207
mezcal
    Century Plant, 42
    Instant Crush, 45
    Red Leather Vermouth, 238

N

nonalcoholic drinks
    Best Person, 221
    Buttermylk Cream Soda, 222
    Greenish, 225
    Nonalcoholic Spritz, 218
    Orxata, 226
    Pandanus Club, 229
    Zebra Wine, 230

P

pear eau de vie: Historically
    Famous, 78
pisco brandy
    Jugo de Selva, 61
    Miraflores Chicha Morada, 62
plum eau de vie: Georgia on My
    Mind, 143
port, tawny: Open Sesame, 204

Q

quince eau de vie: Estonian
    Finnisher, 140

R

rhubarb apéritif: 24 Hours of
    Darkness, 211
rum
    Daiquirita, 31
    Peak Me Up, 119
    Volcan de Masaya, 123
rum, dark
    Camp Pal-o-Mine, 98
    Mercado Mai Thai, 36
    Orange Amargo, 113
    Singularity Dark Vermouth, 239
    Spiced Rum, 133
rum, Guatemalan: Flora Fashion,
    116
rum, white
    Babka Orgeat, 212
    Cola Flower Water, 185
    Dancing Queen, 128
    Miami Stucco Machine, 131
    Orgeat, 47
    Pumpkin Seed Orgeat, 47
    Starlight White Vermouth, 239

S

sake
    Cold as Rice, 196
    Sake with Pineapple, 214
scotch whisky: Pasteis de Nata, 65
sherry, amontillado
    Déjà Brew, 200
    Donostia Askatuta, 57
    Iberian Apéritif, 203
    Orange Amargo, 113
    Volcan de Masaya, 123
sherry, fino
    Autumn & Eve, 70
    Gin & Symphonic, 74
    Green Cameo Vermouth, 238
    Marigold Wine, 157
    Pasteis de Nata, 65
    Seven Mile Mule, 150
sherry, manzanilla: Tinto Naranja,
    110

sherry, PX: Iberian Apéritif, 203
stout: Stout, Stout, Let It All Out,
    177

T
tequila, blanco
    All-Purpose Flower, 28
    Daiquirita, 31
    Family Affair, 32
    Green Cameo Vermouth, 238
    Instant Crush, 45
    Mercado Mai Thai, 36
    Red Leather Vermouth, 238
    Yonge Street, 41
tequila, reposado: Gondwana, 35

V
vermouth
    All-Purpose Flower, 28
    Gin-Gin Donkey Kong, 77
    Gondwana, 35
    Historically Famous, 78
    Instant Crush, 45
    Kale & Nori, 81
    The Kasbah, 82
    Liberation, 53
    Loup-Garou, 183
    Miraflores Chicha Morada, 62
    Orange Amargo, 113
    Peak Me Up, 119
    Sea Basin Bitter, 95
    Smallage, Biggish, 91
    24 Hours of Darkness, 211
    Vieux Boréal, 54
    Westphalia, 105

vermouth, 18%
    Green Cameo Vermouth, 238
    Infrared Red Vermouth, 238
    Master Method, 238
    Mellow Yellow Vermouth, 238
    Nebula Pink Vermouth, 238
    Red Leather Vermouth, 238
    Singularity Dark Vermouth,
        239
    Solar Flare Orange Vermouth,
        239
    Starlight White Vermouth, 239
vermouth, NA
    Nonalcoholic Spritz, 218
    Orange Amargo, 113
    Sea Basin Bitter, 95
vermouth, rosé
    Bajan Apéritif, 188
    Black Forest, 208
vodka
    Balsam Fir Spray, 184
    Cosmonauts 1 & 2, 136
    Double-Double Caesar, 139
    Estonian Finnisher, 140
    Georgia on My Mind, 143
    Grand Palace, 144
    Here Comes the Sun, 147
    Infrared Red Vermouth, 238
    Seven Mile Mule, 150
    Wanna-Bee, 153
    We're Pickle People, 154
vodka, coconut: Coconut Vodka
    with Roses, 112
vodka, orange flavored: Sea Basin
    Bitter, 95

vodka, rose flavored: Sour Roses,
    102

W
whiskey/whisky. *See also*
        Canadian whisky; Irish
        whiskey; scotch whisky
    Betacillin, 174
    Glacial Snout, 180
    Loup-Garou, 183
    Open Sesame, 204
    Stout, Stout, Let It All Out, 177
    Vieux Boréal, 54
whisky, Islay: One Below, 169
whisky, rye
    One Below, 169
    Polar Vortex, 170
    The Unclimbable, 173
wine, fortified
    Black Forest, 208
    Good Vibes Only, 58
wine, NA sparkling: Nonalcoholic
    Spritz, 218
wine, red
    It's Jammy, 195
    Jugo de Selva, 61
wine, rosé
    Bajan Apéritif, 188
    Miami Stucco Machine, 131
wine, sparkling: Sea Basin
    Sbagliato, 88
wine, white
    Cantaloupe Chardonnay, 213
    Marigold Wine, 157